The Barnum & Bailey Greatest Show on Earth.

EAST TIBIAN DWARF | TATTOOED PEOPLE | THE BEARDED LADY | WHAT IS SHE? | THE HUMAN SKYE TERRIER | MOSS HAIRED GIRL | THE SWORD SWALLOWER | THE DOUBLE-BODIED WONDER | THE LIVING SKELETON | THE EGYPTIAN GIANT

THE PEERLESS PRODIGIES OF PHYSICAL PHENOMENA AND GREAT PRESENTATION OF MARVELOUS LIVING HUMAN CURIOSITIES.

PRINTED IN AMERICA

THE WORLD'S LARGEST. GRANDEST. BEST AMUSEMENT INSTITUTION.

PUBLISHERS/EDITORS:	Andrea Juno and V. Vale
ASSISTANT EDITOR:	Catherine Reuther
PRODUCTION & PROOFREADING:	Elizabeth Amon, Elizabeth Borowski, Nicole Castor, Curt Gardner, Mason Jones, Christine Sulewski
CHIEF ADVISOR:	Ken Werner

Paperback: ISBN 0-940642-20-4

15 14 13 12 11 10 9 8 7 6 5

BOOKSTORE DISTRIBUTION: Subco, PO Box 160, Monroe, OR 97456-0160 (800) 274-7826.
FAX: (503) 847-6018
NON-BOOKSTORE DISTRIBUTION: Last Gasp, 2180 Bryant, SF CA 94110 (415) 824-6636
U.K. DISTRIBUTION: Airlift, 26 Eden Grove, London N7 8EL, U.K. (01) 607-5792
SUBSCRIPTIONS: $35 for 3 issues ($45 overseas; $50 for Australia & Asia) $60 Institutions.

Send SASE for catalog: RE/SEARCH PUBLICATIONS
20 Romolo #B
San Francisco CA 94133
(415) 362-1465

Printed in Hong Kong by Colorcraft Ltd.

Front Cover: The lovely Frances O'Conner, born without arms.

Back Cover: Korean Siamese twins joined at the breastbone and Happy Jack Eckert who weighed 739 lbs.

FREAKS: WE WHO ARE NOT AS OTHERS

BY DANIEL P. MANNIX

CONTENTS

"I am convinced that the only people worthy of consideration in this world are the unusual ones. For the common folk are like the leaves of a tree, and live and die unnoticed."

—*The Scarecrow of Oz, from* The Marvelous Land of Oz *by L. Frank Baum*

Dreamland Sideshow Freaks in front of bannerline showing entire company and featuring Mortado, the human fountain—he had holes in his feet and hands that water could be pumped through. This photo was taken in 1931 and features the Fat Lady, Skinny Man, Eko and Iko and many others.

1

We Who Are Not As Others

I have always been interested in freaks—because I am one myself, not in a spectacular way, but different enough from other people to stand out in a crowd. When I was eleven, I was six feet tall. If you happen to be five feet six and wear lifts, this may not seem to be a curse to you, but it was to me. I remember when I was in my late teens I drove Mother to a dancing class to pick up my little sister, who was ten years younger than I. In the class was a great oaf of a kid, head and shoulders taller than the others and as ungainly as an ox with a broken leg. Watching him trying to dance with the little girls, falling over chairs and generally making a nuisance of himself, I asked

Percilla, the monkey-girl, and Emmett, the alligator-skinned man, billed as the "World's Strangest Married Couple."

Photo of unknown hunchback midget taken about 1890.

Mother, "Why don't they put him in a class with children his own age?" Mother gave me a curious look and remarked, "He's the same age as the other children here. That's what you looked like as a child." I've had a fellow feeling for freaks ever since.

I realize that I should not use the word "freak." In these days of euphemisms, freaks are now called "strange people." This is a pity because there are lots of strange people in the world, but only a comparatively few freaks. Also, I don't know of any word that expresses the concept of a dramatic physical deviation from the ordinary as well as "freak." So I'll use it. At least, it is better than the medical term, which is "monster."

If you regard yourself as a normal, healthy-minded person, almost certainly the very idea of a freak is repugnant to you. Although you probably wouldn't go as far as Hitler did and suggest they be killed in gas chambers, still you might very well feel they should be shut up in institutions where no one could see them. After all, think of the effect that seeing a freak could have on a child. Yet children are raised on stories of dwarfs, giants and fairies (all of whom have counterparts and probably their origins in human freaks). It is also true that children, far from feeling an instinctive horror of freaks, are delighted with them. But this is unimportant. It's the principle of the thing.

It is fortunate our ancestors did not take the modern, civilized attitude, for freaks have changed the course of history and greatly contributed to our knowledge of humanity. Bertholde, a hunchbacked dwarf, was probably the best prime minister the Lombards ever had. Jeffrey, a midget, was used as a secret agent by Charles I of England and distinguished himself for having more brains than most secret agents. Bahalul, a court dwarf of Haroun-al Rashid, was famous for his quick wit and resourcefulness. Triboulet, whose head came to a point and wore half an orange peel for a cap, was court jester to Francis I of France and inspired Victor Hugo's famous play *Le Roi s'amuse* and Verdi's immortal *Rigoletto*. Edward the Confessor, one of the greatest English monarchs, was an albino with snow white hair and red eyes. The Emperor Maximilian, who worked his way up from the ranks to the highest position a Roman could attain, was a giant standing between eight and nine feet high. Charles Lockhart, a dwarf who stood forty-two inches high, was three times state treasurer of taxes. I do not even mention such expert showmen as Charles S. Stratton ("General Tom Thumb"), who traveled extensively and acquired a comfortable fortune as did Chang and Eng, the original Siamese twins, Percilla and Emmett (the monkey-girl and alligator-skinned man) and Al Tomaini (a giant) and his wife Jeanie (a half woman), who ran their own side show and retired to Florida on the proceeds. During the last war, midgets made an important contribution as airplane mechanics, for they were the only people small enough to get inside turrets. It would seem to me that all these freaks were happier and more useful than they would be locked up in institutions.

In all reason, I would have to admit that some freaks are so revolting that they should not be allowed in public and would be better off dead. One such monster lived around 600 B.C. and was the slave of a Greek nobleman named Iadmon who lived on Samos. This unfortunate was a hunchback described as having "an enormous head with slit eyes, a long, misshapen countenance, a large mouth and bowed legs." A servant girl meeting him asked in horror, "Are you a baboon?" Because he was cut off from humanity by his revolting appearance, this monster made friends with animals. He told numerous short tales with animal heroes illustrating the weaknesses of people. His stories were so biting and his looks so disgusting that he was finally killed by a mob. His name was Aesop.

Another even more hopeless case was a young girl born a blind deaf-mute. She was given to such outbreaks of fury that it was almost impossible to control her. Instead of taking the sensible course of shutting her up in an institution, her parents and a devoted nurse worked with her constantly. As a result, Helen Keller was able to revolutionize the treatment of the handicapped.

During the three years I worked as a sword-swallower and fire-eater in a carnival side show, I lived and performed with freaks. A good freak would top every outfit on the midway, even the nude posing girls,

Charles Lockhart, who stood 42 inches, served three terms as Texas State Treasurer.

and it's mighty hard to beat sex as an attraction.

Perhaps none of the people in the crowds were normal, but they seemed to regard freaks with the honest interest of kids watching a friend who can wriggle his ears. After the show, a lot of them would cluster around a freak to ask him about his deformity and the freak would answer with the same simple frankness.

Refined individuals have asked me with fascinated disgust, "How can those poor creatures bring themselves to be exhibited?" To understand that, you've got to know how freaks think.

Many freaks have had cruelly unhappy childhoods. Except in a few cases, freakishness is not inherited, so freaks have normal parents. Papa is chain-smoking cigarettes outside the maternity ward when the doctor comes out and gravely tells him that his wife has given birth to a freak. Junior is never going to play on his old football team or go fishing with him ... because junior has two heads. Parents almost invariably react to this news in one of two ways: they develop a violent hatred for the child or they refuse to admit the deformity exists. Both reactions are tough on the little freak.

I once worked with a freak who was billed as the "Pig-faced Boy." He was one of the best-natured persons I've ever known. A hunchbacked dwarf, the boy's face came almost to a point and vaguely suggested an animal's snout. His parents stubbornly refused to acknowledge the boy's deformity and kept insisting that he'd grow out of it.

His earliest memory was of a little girl saying she'd rather leave school than sit next to him. The local kids amused themselves thinking up ways to torture him, and when he heard the dismissal bell ring, he'd begin to cry because he knew the gang would be waiting outside. The gang was always led by the pig-faced boy's brother, who wanted to show the rest of the kids that he despised the dwarf as much as they did.

I realize this contradicts what I have said previously about children being naturally interested in freaks. Of course, everything depends on how the idea of freakishness is presented to them. Children, like adults, have a tendency to attack anything weaker and different than they are; if there is only one white kid in a black school, the black children will attack him, and if there is only one black child in a white school he will also be attacked because he is different. If the children had met Pig-face alone as individuals, they probably would have been curious about him; operating as a mob, they would attack him. Dogs behave the same way. An individual dog may be gentle and friendly, but as a member of a pack he is transformed into a vicious animal.

As soon as he was old enough, Pig-face ran away and joined a carnival. He loved the carny life and made a very good living at it. Ironically, the brother who used to lead the gangs turned out to be a failure. After constantly borrowing money from the pig-faced boy, he finally asked the dwarf to let him act as the little fellow's agent. Pig-face agreed good-naturedly. The brother and his wife traveled with the show and always spoke of the dwarf contemptuously, although they were living off him. I once asked Pig-face why he let them get away with it. "Oh well, he's my brother," said the dwarf gently. "Naturally, you want to do anything you can for your own brother."

To Pig-face, the carnival seemed like paradise. For the first time in his life, his strangeness had become an asset. He knew that the success of the ten-in-one (carny term for the side show) depended largely on him, and he felt a glow of self-respect. He was surrounded by people who admired and even envied him. He told us with amused pride that some ordinary dwarfs with another carny were trying to imitate his appearance by using grease paint and New Skin. "They still look like ordinary people," he told me proudly. "Not me—I *really* look like a pig!"

A good freak is so important that usually the concessionaire won't allow him to appear in the pit with the ordinary acts. The freak lives in a section curtained off from the rest of the tent, and the crowd must pay an additional fee to see him, often much more than they paid to see the rest of the show. This way of handling a freak is called the "blow-off." Many showmen count on the pit acts to pay the running expenses of the ten-in-one and the blow-off to provide the profit. Often the blow-off carries the whole concession and sometimes pays part of the operating expenses of the entire carnival.

Even freaks who are mentally deficient (although very few are) can be much happier in show business than in institutions. I once worked with a family of pinheads (a condition known medically as microcephaly and characterized by a long, rather conical head with a little tuft of hair at the top). Microcephaly is the only type of freakishness that affects the brain, and most pinheads are imbeciles. With our show there were three pinheads, billed as Members of the Savage Nairobi Tribe from Darkest Africa, who used to play together as happily as children. The one named Sally was the star. When the time came for the talker to "turn the tip" (bring the crowd

Elephantiasis of the scrotum.

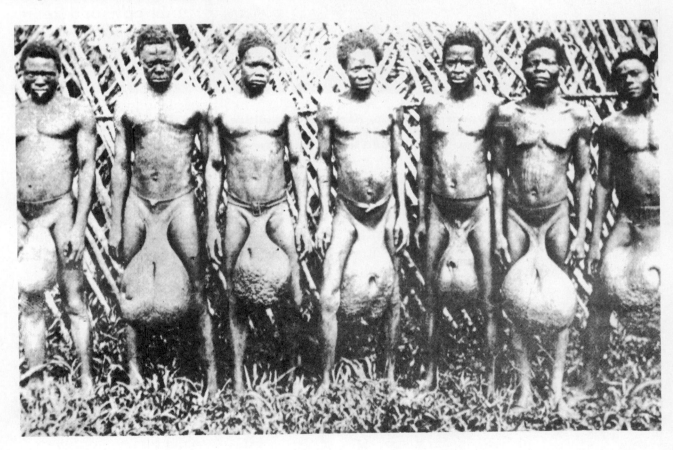

Flip, the frog boy, as he appeared with the Hagenbeck-Wallace Circus Sideshow in 1936. He had a normal-sized body but such tiny feet that in order to get around, he had to hop like a frog. He played a saxophone in his act.

dividuals had complained to the police about exploitation, the little group had been broken up and sent to different institutions. "I finally managed to locate Sally," the talker told me. "She missed her friends and was miserably unhappy. She was sleeping on the floor, the food was terrible, and no one paid any attention to her. I asked if I could get her out by signing papers making myself legally responsible for her. The director told me, 'We don't want her here. She's restless and unhappy, and keeps trying to run away. Besides, we're so overcrowded we've got patients sleeping in the lobby and three to a bed—mentally disturbed patients who have to be institutionalized. Get her out any way you can.' So I signed the papers and got Sally. Now if she misbehaves herself, all I need do is say, 'Sally, I'm going to send you back to the institution,' and she'll run off and hide."

into the tent) he would always call Sally to the "bally platform" (an elevated platform outside the tent) for her come-on dance. Sally's dancing was uproariously amusing, and Sally enjoyed it as much as the crowd. After a minute or so, the talker would shout through his mike, "What you've seen out here ain't even a shinney, come in and watch Sally do the African shimmey." Sally then rushed inside followed by the delighted tip.

Years later, I met the talker again. He told me that because some conscientious in-

Sex is naturally a problem for most freaks and a virtually unsolvable one in an institution, but in show business they can often find a partner. There is a sort of grapevine among the freaks, and no matter how grotesquely they may be deformed, they can almost always find someone sympathetic. When they do, they are always billed as the World's Strangest Married Couple, which greatly increases their billing.

One of the most famous of these freak unions is the marriage of Percilla, the monkey-girl, and Emmett, the alligator-skinned man. They had a remarkable love story.

Both Emmett and Percilla appeared in a side show owned by Mr and Mrs Carl J. Lauther. Nineteen years before, a man and his wife came one night to the Lauther tent with a bundle. The strangers spoke only Portuguese and the Lauthers couldn't understand what they wanted. Finally the man opened the bundle, revealing a baby girl only a few days old. As soon as Lauther saw the child, he knew he was looking at one of the great freaks of all time.

The baby was completely covered with long, black hair. Doctors call this condition "excessive hirsuties" and it is extremely rare. The Lauthers adopted the baby. The parents stayed with the show for a time to comply with a law stating that they had to make sure that the child was not being cruelly treated. Then they left. They never returned. The Lauthers raised the little girl as their own daughter and named her Percilla.

When Percilla was old enough to appear in the show, she caused a sensation. Being smart showmen, the Lauthers got Percilla a young chimpanzee named Joanna. The girl and the ape became fast friends and traveled everywhere together. When the carnival played Cuba, the natives turned out by the thousands to see the "monkey-girl who lives with apes."

One night, a tall, elegantly dressed woman arrived at the carnival in a sleek, black car. Heavily veiled, she sat through show after show, never taking her eyes from Percilla. After the last show, she spoke to the Lauthers.

The woman was Madam Obrea. She lived in a huge house outside Havana with no companions other than a number of giant apes. The house and grounds were surrounded by a high wall and a moat. At night, fierce dogs were turned loose to keep away visitors. Madam Obrea told the Lauthers that she wanted to adopt Percilla. She promised to give the girl the best possible education and settle a considerable sum of money on her.

Percilla refused to go. She liked the carnival life and loved her foster parents. The Lauthers were in a quandary. Percilla was a valuable attraction, and the Lauthers were afraid of being accused of holding the girl in order to exploit her. They knew Madam Obrea could give Percilla advantages they could not. Also, there was another consideration. Percilla had two sets of teeth in her upper jaw, one set behind the other. Some of the teeth in the front set were coming through the gums. To correct this problem, a very elaborate operation would have to be performed on the girl's mouth, and the Lauthers did not have enough money for the surgeon's bill. Madam Obrea had offered to pay for the operation. The Lauthers told Percilla they thought she should accept the wealthy Cuban's offer.

Percilla was miserable. She distrusted Madam Obrea's attachment to apes and suspected the woman's motives. Yet she trusted the Lauthers and had always followed their advice. It was a tough decision for a seventeen-year-old girl to make.

With the show was a young fellow named Emmett. From throat to waist his body was covered by a rough, corrugated growth that looked somewhat like the scales of an alligator. This condition is called "ichthyosis." It is a thickening of the epidermis and is not dangerous or contagious.

Emmett was billed as the "alligator-skinned boy," and for some time he had been

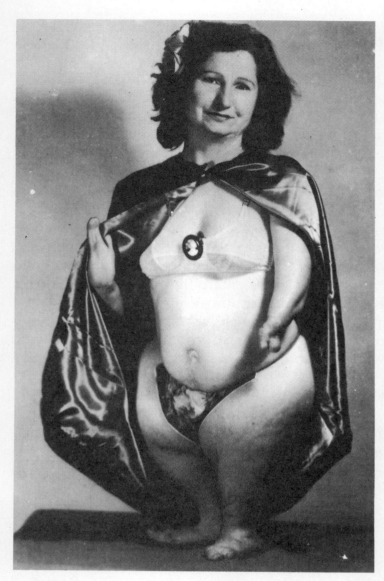

Mignon, the "Penguin Girl."

eloped. But Carl Lauther had not been a showman for thirty years for nothing. He promptly billed the newlyweds as the World's Strangest Couple. The sensation they caused packed the show, and a few months later Percilla had enough money for her operation.

Percilla and Emmett now own a pleasant house in Florida where they spend their winters. The couple enjoys the gypsy life of the carnival and travels with shows in the summer. Emmett's ichthyosis developed to such a degree that even without the tie-in with Percilla, he would have become one of the biggest attractions in carnivals. In addition to being famous, Emmett and Percilla became one of the best-liked couples in show business. They have two children who are perfectly normal and grew up under canvas proud of their famous parents.

If you have read this far, it is possible that you don't share the popular dislike of freaks. If so, don't feel ashamed. It is a trait you share with Victor Hugo, Shakespeare, Cervantes, Toulouse-Lautrec (who was a freak himself), Walter Scott, Edgar Allan Poe and, in the world of art, Francisco Rizi, Giovanni Bologna, Leonardo de Vinci, Velasquez and Trevisani. In music there is Verdi and Dick Deadeye in Gilbert and Sullivan's *H.M.S. Pinafore*. Also, you will be one of the millions of people who have delighted in the Munchkins in MGM's *The Wizard of Oz*, starring Judy Garland. It is even possible that you have read with pleasure Tolkien's books about hobbits. So don't give up hope. It may even be that you're normal and the people who profess to find freaks revolting are the distorted ones.

in love with Percilla. Percilla had a slender, graceful figure and a remarkably lovely voice which seems to be a characteristic of hirsuties. At that time, Emmett's ichthyosis had not progressed far enough to make the boy a headliner with the show. So Emmett had always regarded Percilla with the respectful admiration of an extra for a star.

When Percilla told him that she might have to leave the carnival, the boy broke down and asked her to marry him. Somewhat to the dismay of the Lauthers, they

2

Small is Beautiful

People have always been fascinated by miniatures, whether bonsai or Pekinese. Why, it is hard to say. Maybe because we can both dominate and protect something small, and this satisfies a parental instinct. It is the reason why pets are so popular. Of course, you can satisfy a parental instinct by having children, but children make very unsatisfactory toys (as every parent knows). Women, especially, have always been delighted by little people and want to treat them as children—which little people hate. A woman picked up Michael Dunn, the dwarf actor who first won recognition in *The Ballad of the Sad Cafe*, and petted him like a child. Dunn bit her. The only midget I know of that accepted this attitude good-naturedly was Barnum's General Tom Thumb, who toured Europe and America in the middle of the last century.

Twenty-four midgets in Chaffer's Wonder Midgets troupe, 1938. The man posing with them is 6 feet 10 inches tall.

The Doll Family.

In England alone, Tom was kissed by over a million women. Today, most midgets would consider this degrading, but Tom didn't care. He left England with 150,000 pounds, bought a big estate in Bridgeport and got a steam yacht and a stable of thoroughbreds.

Especially intriguing is the idea of a whole race of little people living in some faraway country with everything scaled down to their size. This conception has charmed writers from Homer to Tolkien. It is particularly appealing to children because they can identify with such a community. When Dorothy arrives in Oz, she immediately meets the Munchkins, who are "no taller than Dorothy herself." No child and few adults can resist reading what happens next. However, I'm luckier than most because I've met a Munchkin

and not only a Munchkin but the coroner who pronounced the Wicked Witch of the East dead in the unforgettable words "as coroner I must aver, I thoroughly examined her, and she's not only merely dead, she's really most sincerely dead." There are not many people who can boast that they've had lunch with a four-foot coroner who's checked the corpus delicti of a witch.

In private life, the coroner is Meinhardt Raabe, now a horticulturist but formerly an actor, lecturer and accountant. You probably know him best as Oscar the Weiner Man. For many years his cheerful face ornamented the packages of sausages manufactured by the Oscar Mayer Meat Company. Mr Raabe isn't young anymore, but he's still very active. Midgets seem to age less than big people, perhaps because they don't have so much weight to drag around.

I asked Mr Raabe what it was like to live in a world where everything was outsized—where climbing into a chair was an effort, turning a door handle impossible, elevator buttons were out of reach and using a toilet was a gymnastics feat. "Being little is fun," said Mr Raabe cheerfully. "I'm glad I'm not big."

Meinhardt Raabe was born and brought up on a farm in Wisconsin. Like all pituitary midgets (midgets whose small size is due to malfunctioning of the pituitary gland), he was a normal baby. He grew normally until he was four, but from then on he only grew a quarter of an inch a year. For some reason, his pituitary gland had ceased to function normally, and at nineteen, he was only forty-six inches tall.

In psychiatric studies of little people, much has been written about their traumatic experiences: how they are rejected by their parents as "devil's children" and ridiculed by their schoolmates. Raabe does not remember any such experience.

"At school, there was some horseplay, but it was good-natured. My parents were mainly concerned with how I was to earn a living as I was too small to do much farm work, although I always milked the cows. Both my parents and I thought I was unique. There didn't seem to be any place for me."

In 1934, some neighbors returned from a trip to the Chicago World's Fair and told Raabe that there was a whole midget village there with dozens of little men and women no bigger than he was. Raabe left for Chicago on the next train. The midget village was under the direction of Nate Eagle, the famous impresario who specialized in handling midgets. When Raabe walked through the gate, Eagle took one look at him and said, "You're hired." "I didn't know what he was talking about," Raabe explained.

At that time there were about three hundred midgets in America who often exhibited themselves in "midget villages" where the houses, furniture, street lamps and even animals were scaled down to their size. Walking into one of these miniature communities was like entering fairyland. Actually, midgets do not especially like to live with members of their own kind. Most prefer to show that they can compete with normal-sized people in the regular world. They dislike using small tables, chairs and other articles as it makes them feel like children. Although having virtually every article of clothing especially made is murderously expensive, nearly all midgets insist on doing it rather than wear children's clothing. Nor will they order child-sized portions of food in restaurants even if they can't eat the regular meals (although I must say the midgets I've known ate like normal-sized people; their metabolism seems to be higher). However, since the public wanted to see midget villages and since in those days show business was almost the only way a midget could earn a living, they went along with the idea.

Raabe joined the troupe and met such famous midgets as Buddie Thompson, the Del Rios and the Doll family. Raabe is naturally a good talker and soon was acting as MC for the troupe. He earned enough money to go to college; he has a B.A. from the University of Wisconsin and later got a master's at Drexel Institute. While at college, he worked as a page at a hotel, greeting the guests. "Every dignitary in Wisconsin contributed to my education—a nickel at a time," he joked. After graduating, he tried to get a job as an accountant and then in civil service, but was turned down because of his size. Most people find it hard to believe that even though a midget is no bigger than a child he has the brains of an adult.

At that time, a midget named Johnny Roventini was doing very well for himself as a sort of trademark for Philip Morris. Johnny had been working as a page boy in the Hotel New Yorker when an advertising man staying at the hotel heard Johnny paging people and had an idea. Soon millions of people were listening to Johnny's voice on the radio: "Call for Philip Mor-ris!" Johnny made numerous public appearances in his page boy uniform, and the demand for him was so great that over a period of years there were fifteen "Johnnies" touring the country. Johnny, who had been making fifteen dollars a week at the hotel plus tips, soon was making fifty thousand dollars a year. It was Johnny's success that inspired Raabe to suggest a similar deal with Oscar Mayer which also proved highly successful.

While working as "Oscar the Wiener Man," Raabe heard though the "little people's underground" that MGM was doing *The Wizard of Oz* and needed midgets to play the Munchkins. Raabe was so excited that he got a leave of absence for two months from Oscar Mayer and went to Los Angeles. "I'd have taken the job for nothing if I'd had to," he explained.

Leo Singer, whose midget troupe called the Singer Midgets was world-famous, had been given the job of supplying the Munchkins. Singer had become interested in midgets many years before in Vienna, when he took his little daughter to a fair where there was a midget performer. The little girl was so delighted with the midget that she ignored all the other exhibitions. Singer guessed that other children would feel the same way and set about organizing a midget troupe. It was enormously successful. At the time of the MGM picture (1939) Singer had only twenty-eight midgets and had been forced to tour the country with two buses collecting others. He managed to find 128. They were housed in a special hotel in Culver City where they had quite a gay time. According to Judy Garland, "they'd get smashed every night and the next morning Metro would have to catch them with butterfly nets." Raabe says the story is ridiculous. "We were much too tired after a day's work on the set for such nonsense."

Shooting the Munchkin sequence took two weeks. Because of his experience as an MC, Raabe got one of the few talking parts. The make-up was devised by Adrian, who was famous for his technique. Each Munchkin's make-up was different, and after putting it on, Adrian had the actor photographed so he could match it next time.

Raabe returned to Oscar Mayer after the famous sequence was completed. When the war came, he tried to join the air force as a tail gunner but was turned down. "I heard you needed small men as tail gunners," he

protested. "Not *that* small," retorted the recruiting sergeant. So Raabe was forced to stay with the advertising business.

In 1946, Raabe married a pretty, young midget girl who was a dancer in vaudeville. The marriage has been most successful. They have no children. Since two midgets will often have a child of normal size (a notable exception is the Swensen family, which has given birth to midgets for three generations), the child must frequently be delivered by a Caesarean operation which, because of the baby's size, can be dangerous to the little mother.

When he reached thirty, Raabe began to grow more rapidly. This often happens with midgets; the reason is unknown. It usually ruins the midget's career in show business and so was once considered a disaster. There is an old story of two midgets who had a feud. One would steal the other's cane every day and cut a little off the bottom. The midget thought he was growing and in despair committed suicide. All I can say is that he was a mighty stupid midget to be fooled like that.

Raabe became four feet nine inches tall, but he was not unduly upset. "During the war, when there was a manpower shortage, midgets showed they could handle almost any job an average-sized person can," he told me. "In some jobs they were superior—like working in the wing of a plane where the space is so confined a normal-sized man can't get in. So the prejudice against hiring little people has largely disappeared."

I have heard many gruesome stories of midgets being attacked by malicious children or depraved men. "I only had two such experiences," Raabe said. "Once, in Chicago, a boy tried to snatch the briefcase I was carrying. Luckily, I had exceptionally strong hands from milking so I grabbed his finger and twisted it. The boy hadn't expected any resistance from a midget and was so frightened he ran. I didn't come out of the other encounter so well. In Michigan, another boy jumped me outside the theater door and attempted to rob me. He hit me in the face and knocked one of my teeth through my cheek. Someone came along and the boy ran off. I had to have my cheek stitched up before I could go on again in the show."

Raabe told me that there are few midgets in show business today. "Those who are, are mainly in Hollywood working as stunt men," he said to my surprise. "They double for children. In many movies with child stars, the script calls for the child to perform some stunt or take some risk which neither the parents nor the Society for the Prevention of Cruelty to Children will permit. So a midget stunt man is called in. They make a good living. But midget villages are a thing of the past."

During the filming of Peter Benchley's best seller *Jaws*, the producer hired a midget stunt man whose job it was to be lowered in a cage as bait for the shark. The idea was that the midget would make the shark look bigger. The shark attacked the cage so savagely he tore it to pieces, and the little stunt man barely made it to the surface. "We'll have to shoot that scene over," said the director casually. "Nothing doing!" returned the midget firmly, and the idea had to be abandoned.

I suppose it is a good thing that midgets don't have to depend on show business for a living, but I used to enjoy the midget villages. Some were very elaborate, having baby elephants which the midgets rode, midget orchestras, which I recall as being excellent, and midget craftsmen who did fine miniature work so delicate a normal human finger would have been too clumsy for it.

There is no rigid definition of how small

a person has to be to qualify as a midget or a dwarf, but I would say under four and a half feet. Medically, any small person is called a "dwarf," but in popular parlance a dwarf is deformed and a midget is not. This is a distinction carefully observed by the little people themselves. At one time, the worst insult you could bestow on a midget was to call him a "dwarf." I have been told that formerly a midget would hardly speak to a dwarf—he was considered so inferior. However, this feeling has largely disappeared, especially since the creation of the Little People of America, an organization embracing both midgets and dwarfs.

Martin S. Weinberg of Rutgers did an analysis of the Little People of America with their full cooperation. He was especially interested in how a group confronted by a social stigma can overcome it. This problem is not, of course, confined to freaks. Members of certain religions, racial, ethnic and social groups also suffer from it, but nowhere is it seen so clearly as with freaks. Some of the groups are large enough that the members can find companionship, or, by changing their way of life, the stigmatized individuals can more or less join the majority group. This is virtually impossible with freaks. They cannot change their appearance and there are too few of them to form the equivalent of a Jewish community or a Negro community or a "Little Italy." So it is with them that the difficulties of a socially ostracized group can best be studied.

The Little People of America was founded in 1957 with twenty-seven members. It now has 1,500 little people on its mailing list. The little people meet several times a year to make new friends, discuss job opportunities and learn how others have coped with the problem of being small.

Dr Weinberg came to the conclusion that

little people are most unhappy when they refuse to accept the fact that they are different from others. He pointed out that Alcoholics Anonymous is unable to help a drunkard who refuses to admit that he is a drunkard. The little person must face the fact that he will never be regarded as anything but a freak by the majority of people. If he continues to fight this attitude, he will grow embittered and resentful.

A good example of a little person who was miserably unhappy until he learned to accept himself for what he was is Herve Villechaise, a French midget. Until he was sixteen, Herve and his parents spent a small fortune on medical and hormone treatments both in France and the United States. They were not successful, and Herve never grew more than three feet nine inches. When Herve was forced to recognize the truth, he went on a binge that lasted for several years, drinking heavily, chasing (often successfully) girls and living in the Latin Quarter, where he tried to paint like Toulouse-Lautrec. As a result, he developed a liver condition and now drinks nothing but soda water. For a surprisingly long time, Herve regarded himself—as did Meinhardt Raabe—as unique, and it was only after he had met some other midgets that he realized he wasn't alone in the world. Then in a Parisian paper he read an ad by a motion picture company which needed a midget. After considerable soul-searching, Herve applied for the job. That started him on an acting career. His latest picture is *The Man With the Golden Gun*, a James Bond film. He is married to a normal-sized girl.

Dolly Regan, who is herself a dwarf and

Dolletta, shown here with her two normal-sized children, both born by Caesarean operations.

billed as the Ossified Girl because of a condition resembling a sort of painless arthritis, told me of a little person she knows who is deformed in such a way that he cannot possibly do any sort of work and must either be institutionalized or exhibit himself. Since institutionalizing is regarded by most mentally active people as a living death, he travels in side shows. "But he hates the people who come to look at him," Dolly told me. "You can see it in his face all during his act. It's a pity, for he's making a good living, everyone with the show likes him, and he could have a happy life." Dolly added that this is one of the very few cases she has met in forty years of show business in which a freak has refused to adjust.

Freaks, like nearly all members of a minority group, tend to accept the standards of the majority. For many years, Negroes did this. Looked down on because of the color of their skin, they tried to make themselves into white people. Negro magazines were full of advertisements for bleaches, hair straighteners and claims by quack doctors who pretended to make noses smaller and lips thinner. It was not until Negroes decided that "black is beautiful" and took pride in appearing as they are that they achieved peace of mind. In somewhat the same way, many little people are proud of their uniqueness; they feel that they can perform certain jobs better than normal people, like selling products and working in show business. Even so, they often have problems.

The directors of the Little People of America found that many dwarfs and midgets at the conventions are so delighted with being among people like themselves for the first time that they are inclined to rush into impulsive marriages. On the other hand, if they are not immediately accepted by the group, they suffer from a much stronger feeling of rejection than if they were excluded by ordinary people. They cannot understand why "their own people" don't like them, but as with normal individuals, some little people have likeable personalities and some do not, while some are better-looking than others. Although many marriages have come about through meetings at the conventions, the LPA stresses that it is not a lonely hearts organization and urges members not to attend with the idea that they are sure to find a partner. On the other hand, most marriages between little people are lasting. To put it bluntly, the little people realize they have a limited choice of partners, and if they lose one mate, they may never get another.

All little people are troubled by the problem of having children. Like ordinary people, most want children but, in addition to the complication of delivery, there is a chance that the child may be small like the parents. One little man told Dr Weinberg, "It rather shook me to realize there were quite a few couples who had married, had dwarfed children and did not think too much of the moral obligations . . . Has one the right to produce a child when the chances are fifty-fifty . . . that it will be dwarfed? Two years ago, my answer was no. Now I am less sure."

A number of little people solve this problem by adopting dwarf children. Many parents who have such children refuse to keep them, and adopting couples generally will not take a deformed child. A dwarf couple who adopts such a child can give him love and understanding which is sometimes difficult for normal parents to do.

So far, I have bracketed dwarfs and midgets because of their height, but in some respects they have quite different problems. Dwarfs may be the result of several different conditions, such as rickets, cretinism or a thyroid condition, whereas midgets are almost always the result of a malfunctioning of the pituitary gland. As a result, dwarfs are born deformed while midgets may be quite normal until they are several years old. It is very difficult to classify the different types of dwarfs because, like all freaks, dwarfs are comparatively rare, although they are far more common than midgets. They occur about once in every forty thousand births, so statistically there are about sixty-five thousand in the world today. Even specialists in bone dysplasia seldom have the opportunity to study more than two or three. Hence, "nomenclature is chaotic," to quote Dr Victor A. McKusick of Johns Hopkins, who has attempted to classify the various types. By far the most common is the chondrodystrophic dwarf, the classical prototype of a dwarf. Chondrodystrophia was once called "fetal rickets," because it twists and bends the bone structure. It is also found in animals, such as the English bulldog, and is often hereditary, although the offspring of two dwarfs seldom live. A chondrodystrophic dwarf has bandy legs, short arms, a normal body, a large head with a protruding forehead and a broad, saddle-shaped nose. Most dwarfs are normal mentally and some have even been geniuses.

Although I would be inclined to say that there have been more brilliant dwarfs than midgets, dwarfs have always had a hard time of it. Whereas midgets have usually been regarded with respect, dwarfs have nearly always been treated with ridicule because of their deformity. For centuries they were kept as court jesters by kings and nobles and as such served a useful purpose. Because he was not regarded as really human, it was beneath a king's dignity to take umbrage at anything the jester said, so the dwarf was the only person in the court who could speak openly. As a result, he was often used as a mouthpiece by officials and also had the job of telling the monarch any bad news when no one else dared to incur the royal wrath. So important did the position of jester become that when not enough dwarfs were available, normal men who feigned insanity were employed since lunatics were also allowed to commit *lese majesty*. Some of these court dwarfs were extremely clever men and have become legends.

One such dwarf was Bahalul, who was jester to Caliph Haroun-al-Rashid of *Arabian Nights* fame. In addition to being a dwarf, Bahalul played it safe by also pretending to be an idiot and was probably the originator of the "little moron" jokes. He claimed that once he was on a sinking ship, but he saved himself by grabbing the anchor. He boasted of standing in front of a mirror with his eyes closed so he could see what he looked like when asleep. He undertook to keep a horse alive without feeding it and swore that he would have succeeded if the horse hadn't died. Once when Haroun asked him to describe a new palace being built by a wealthy noble, Bahalul brought to him a brick from a building as a sample.

In spite of pretending to be a fool, Bahalul had a quick wit. When the caliph humorously bestowed on him the title of "King of the Apes and Asses," he declined, remarking, "I am not ambitious enough to rule over all your majesty's subjects." However, like many comics he went too far.

The caliph married a beautiful young princess, and during the wedding feast, Haroun ordered Bahalul to display his ingenuity by committing the most heinous crime possible and then justifying it by an excuse that was even worse. Apparently defeated, Bahalul slunk out of the room. A few minutes later, the caliph leaped from his cushions with a yell. Bahalul had sneaked up behind the king and "goosed" him. Instantly, Bahalul cried, "Pardon me, my lord, your behind is so round and plump I thought I was goosing the queen." Haroun admitted that Bahalul had won, but banished him from the court, ordering him never to set foot on Persian soil again. Bahalul went to Egypt, but returned when he thought the caliph had calmed down. As he presented himself at court, Haroun shouted, "Didn't I forbid you ever to set foot on Persian soil?" "You did," replied the jester, "and I have followed your majesty's orders." Removing his shoes, he showed that they were full of Egyptian earth.

No one knows who the first dwarf jester was, but Pepi I of Egypt (2600 B.C.) had a dwarf jester named Danga. The pharaoh was fond of saying, "I am the gods' Danga: they must find me as ridiculous as I find my jester." The Egyptians delighted in dwarfs, and they appear in numerous paintings. They even had a dwarf god, Bes, who looked after misfits and people whom the other gods ignored.

The Romans also were fascinated by dwarfs. There was a special slave market, the Forum Morionium, where they were sold. Plutarch complained, "People pass over beautiful slave girls and boys to buy deformities." Martial told of buying a dwarf he thought was a cretin to serve as a clown and then, finding the child had normal intelligence, demanded his money back. Augustus Caesar had a dwarf named Lucius and was so affected when Lucius died that he had a statue made of him with precious stones for eyes. Domitian maintained a small army of dwarf gladiators and made them fight in the arena.

One of the last of the dwarf jesters was Perkeo, jester to Charles-Phillippe, elector of the Palatine, in the early part of the eighteenth century. He specialized in practical jokes, sometimes falling on a table and rolling himself up in the tablecloth along with all the dishes. It was said of Perkeo that "he was the smallest man in the kingdom with the greatest thirst." He drank twenty liters of wine a day. Before the great tun of Heidelberg (which holds 140,000 liters) there is a wooden statue of him. Perkeo asked that after his death he be buried under the spigot of the tun with his mouth open, but whether this request was granted is doubtful. Beside the carved figure is a clock with a string hanging out. If you pull the string, a fox's brush flies out and hits you in the face. Perkeo is still playing tricks.

A number of famous men were reputed to have been dwarfs: Procopius the historian, Croesus (so rich his name has become a synonym for vast wealth), Gregory of Tours, Pepin le Bref, Charles II and Albert the Grand. Some writers call Attila the Hun a dwarf, but this is probably not true. The Huns were a naturally small people and bowlegged from much riding. Attila himself had court dwarfs whom he used as jesters at banquets. A Roman visitor relates that while the courtiers were howling with laughter at the dwarfs' antics, Attila himself never so much as smiled, continuing to eat his frugal meal of horse meat and mare's milk.

The question of whether central Europe should be Protestant or Catholic was nearly decided by two dwarfs. In 1461, the King of Hungary met with the King of Bohemia to debate the question. Not being able to agree, they decided to arm their court dwarfs and let them fight it out. Unfortunately, the onlookers got so excited that they joined the fight and the whole affair ended in a general riot.

Dwarfs are often remarkably strong. Michael Dunn, the dwarf actor, was walking with a young girl when a man tried to pull the girl into a car, thinking that the little Dunn would be helpless to protect her. Dunn broke his leg and, leaving him in the gutter, took the girl home and then called police. David Ritchie, who became a hermit in Peebleshire, Scotland to escape public ridicule, was able to drive his fist through the bottom of a barrel. Walter Scott visited "bow'd Davie" in 1797 and found him so interesting and intelligent he wrote a novel about him, *The Black Dwarf*. Because of their strength, monarchs sometimes used dwarfs as executors. Cut off from the human race by their deformities, they were dependent on the king's favor and so could be depended upon more than ordinary men. In addition, their tongues were cut out and red hot wires run through their eardrums to render them deaf and dumb so they could not repeat the secrets of the court. Dwarfs who survived this treatment were extremely valuable. In *Don Juan*, Byron speaks of two dwarf guards saying, "They were misshapen Pygmies, deaf and dumb, monsters who cost a no less monstrous sum." Such dwarfs dressed elegantly, and were regarded with awe and respect. Lady Montague calls them "devils bedaubed with diamonds."

Because of the superstitious regard in which they were held, it was occasionally possible for a dwarf to rise to a position of great importance if he were shrewd enough to capitalize on his grotesque appearance and the stupidity of the nobility. This is in sharp contrast to the situation that existed only a few years ago in this country, when a little person could not become an accountant because of prejudice. Perhaps the most brilliant dwarf on record was Bertholde. Bertholde was not merely a dwarf; he was a monster. He was about four feet high, waddled on bandy legs and was hunchbacked. But it was his face that most shocked people. His mouth stretched from ear to ear. His nose was mashed flat. His lower lip hung over his chin. Two teeth projected from his mouth like the tusks of a wild boar.

He was born in a small village near Verona some time in the middle of the sixth century to a peasant family. His parents used to hire him out to frighten naughty children into obedience. However, soon he became famous for his quick wit and on Sundays would put on little skits for the amusement of the serfs. When he grew older, his parents found it increasingly difficult to support him as he was too deformed to work in the fields and they had ten other offspring. So Bertholde decided to go to the court of Alboin, king of the Lombards, and seek his fortune. He arrived when the king and his courtiers were at dinner, and after a moment of dumfounded silence, the whole court burst into howls of laughter. The ladies pelted him with food, and the men shouted to their hounds to harry him around the room.

"What do you want here?" asked the king between sobs of laughter.

"To see a king. I thought a monarch would have more sense than to ridicule a cripple, but now I realize you are as stupid as anyone else."

Nobody talked like that to a sixth-century king. Alboin ordered the dwarf hanged.

Bertholde accepted the sentence calmly. He only requested that he be allowed to pick the tree. Alboin granted the plea amid more shouts of laughter, and the guards dragged the dwarf away.

An hour later, the captain of the guards returned scratching his head. "Your majesty, the monster has selected a tree. It's a sapling two feet high. He says that he's willing to wait until it grows. What shall I do?"

After thinking it over, Alboin decided to keep Bertholde as his court jester. Ten years later, Bertholde was prime minister and the most powerful man in the country.

Many stories of Bertholde's ingenuity are told. Once he bet the king that in one day he could turn all the women in the kingdom against the handsome monarch. As women were revolted by the dwarf's hideous appearance while the king was extremely popular, he accepted the wager. Bertholde accomplished the feat by circulating the rumor that Alboin had passed a law permitting a man to have seven wives. A mob of infuriated women stormed the palace, and the king had to call out the army to disperse them. In a rage, Alboin ordered Bertholde sent to the public executioner for a whipping. Bertholde asked that his head be spared so the king added a postscript to the order, "Save the head." Bertholde marched off, followed by a guard of soldiers. At the prison, Bertholde explained to the executioner that he was the head of the procession and the worthy official was to whip the guards. This was done and the king, hearing of the turnabout, not only recovered fully from his rage but let the dwarf off. After all, it hadn't been the king who was whipped by Bertholde's prank.

The queen hated Bertholde and made several attempts to have him murdered. She obtained a pair of huge, vicious dogs especially trained to attack any small, moving object. Bertholde knew about the dogs and made his preparations. While he was crossing a courtyard, the queen set the dogs on him, but Bertholde had a rabbit hidden under his jacket and turned it loose. The dogs took off after the rabbit. On another occasion, the queen armed her ladies-in-waiting with clubs and then sent for Bertholde. The women were ordered to beat him to death with the story to be given out later that the ladies were merely indulging in some rough horseplay common

in the court and had hit a little too hard. Bertholde walked into the room unsuspectingly but when the women rushed at him he instantly shouted, "Aha! I see the lady whom I found in bed with the king is about to strike me first!" The women stopped nonplussed, and Bertholde escaped.

Before Bertholde died, he made a famous will. In it he left a venereal infection he had acquired to the queen, the churches of Lombardy to the bishop ("he will find them interesting because I know he has never been in one") and his filth to a rival courtier ("after eating so much of the king's, I'm sure that he'll welcome a change"). To the king he left the power "to hold the balance between the rich and the poor with an even hand, never to pronounce sentence in anger, to think before he speaks, and to stop all tricks and quibbles of the court."

It was the Scandinavians who first started to treat dwarfs as something more than clowns. There was a good reason for this. In the isolated communities, cut off from each other by the great fjords, there was considerable inbreeding, and dwarfs were common (the same is true among certain Pennsylvania Dutch communities who intermarry for religious reasons). The Norse dwarfs were described as sometimes noble (such as Alberich, Siegfried's faithful follower) and sometimes villainous (like Rumpelstiltskin), and many were expert craftsman. Because of their size dwarfs were handicapped as farmers or sailors but could be smiths or metal workers. One well-known dwarf craftsman was Wybrand Lolkes, who was born in Holland in 1733. He was an expert watchmaker and supported not only himself but his parents and seven brothers and sisters. Unfortunately, Lolkes overextended his business and got into financial troubles. Undiscouraged, he went to England and exhibited himself together with his wife, a woman of normal height. Although Lolkes himself was only slightly over two feet high, he was remarkably agile and could spring from the floor onto the seat of a chair. After making enough to redeem his affairs, he returned to Holland and continued his trade. Many dwarfs also worked in mines, where their short stature was an advantage. In legend, dwarfs are frequently associated with mining. Snow White's seven dwarfs worked in a mine.

Unquestionably, the most famous dwarf in history was Toulouse-Lautrec (1864-1901). Toulouse-Lautrec was the son of a nobleman who married his first cousin. The boy was not born a dwarf but suffered from psknodysostosis, a weakness of the limbs, probably as the result of inbreeding. As a child, he was forced to walk with a cane. At the age of fourteen, he fell from a chair and fractured his left femur which never healed properly. He still tried to walk and play like a normal boy and later fractured his right femur falling into a ditch. His deformed legs made him so small that when Jose Ferrer played the part in *Moulin Rouge* he had to walk on his knees. Because he was ashamed to appear in society, Toulouse spent his time in circuses and cheap cafes, making sketches for the now famous lithographs of the performers. At least according to legend, he led an unhappy life as he was much attracted to pretty women who looked down on him because of his deformity. In this respect he resembled the English poet Alexander Pope, who was also deformed, although he could not properly be called a dwarf. He developed a passion for the beautiful Lady Mary Montague, and when she laughed at him, Pope became so embittered it poisoned his whole life.

Largely due to the Scandinavian influence, in the Middle Ages dwarfs ceased to be regarded as clowns and were treated with respect. Later, the public ironically returned to the ancient attitude, and for years almost the only occupation a dwarf could find was as a clown in the circus. At one time, virtually every circus had a troupe of dwarf clowns. One of the most famous—and one whom I had the pleasure of knowing—was Alva Evans, who was married to Tiny LaVonda. LaVonda was not only a dwarf but had no legs, her feet being directly attached to her body. She was fifteen inches high and weighed twenty-one pounds. They were a devoted couple, Alva pushing his tiny wife everywhere in a little wheelchair. Both of them were fine people, and everyone who knew them liked and admired the spunky couple.

Another highly talented dwarf is Pete Terhune, who has been with Ward Hall, the famous side-show impresario, for twenty-five years. Pete is so versatile that he is a whole side-show in himself. He can do fire-eating, walk up a ladder of sharp swords in his bare feet, walk on broken glass, throw knives and do a clown routine. He works under the stage name of Pooh-Bah (the "lord-high everything else," from Gilbert and Sullivan's *The Mikado*).

Only a few dwarfs were able to make their way outside of show business. One was Charles Lockhart, who was elected to the position of state treasurer of Texas three times. Mr Lockhart stood only forty-two inches high. Another dwarf who was able to win out above all prejudice was Lee Kitchens, who became a highly successful engineer and is past president of the Little People of America. Mr Kitchens married another dwarf and they fly their own plane.

One of the most successful dwarfs is Jean Brisse-Saint-Macary, a noted French jurist, mountain-climber and crack pistol shot, who at seventy-one is now retired. Brisse is the son of a general in the French army who was so shocked by the child's appearance that he insisted on forcing him to be normal. Jean was strapped in bed and subjected to excruciatingly painful treatments intended to soften his bones and stretch him. Naturally, they were unsuccessful.

In school, his fellow pupils made his life hell, and even the teachers despised him. He recalls one telling him, "Brisse, you are abnormal, an imbecile and a dangerous being, but I will break you." At last, the desperate child tried to kill himself by jumping from the roof of the school. As he jumped, a priest associated with the school caught his leg. "We were both weeping," Brisse recalls. However, he graduated and went on to law school. Later, he became a vice-president of the Congress of French Public Notaries and was a counselor at the French Ministry of Justice. He is a recognized expert on rural economy.

Once he was followed by a group of youngsters who stoned him. Brisse finally turned and slapped one. The boy's mother rushed out of a doorway and knocked the dwarf down, cursing him. On another occasion, he was sitting at a table in an outside cafe when four girls sat down beside him. After a few words, they stated clearly that they wanted to sleep with a dwarf as a new experience. Brisse told them he was a law official, and the girls fled.

Brisse is married to a normal woman and has a normal daughter. He also had a son who was a dwarf, but who died as a child. He is now writing a book hoping to make people realize the problems of being different from others.

Being a romanticist, I sometimes wonder if dwarfs did not have it better in the Middle Ages, when they could play up their deformities to become the confidants of kings and exert enormous influence, but I doubt if the dwarfs would agree with me. They would rather be accepted as human beings than be semi-supernatural, even if being a semi-supernatural monster generally pays much better.

Tiny LaVonda, born with no body below the waist, seated on the lap of her husband, clown Alva Evans, 1947. She gave birth to a baby in the spring of 1951 but it died within a few hours.

3 The Mighty Midgets

Midgets should always have had it easier than dwarfs. As dwarfs are deformed, they tend to revolt the average person (unless they are treated as clowns), while people have always been delighted with midgets. The ladies who were eager to kiss Tom Thumb would have shuddered at the idea of kissing a dwarf. For some midgets, at

Lia Graf, the German midget who sat in J. P. Morgan's lap. She returned to Germany and was gassed by Hitler.

least, the fact that they are identical to a normal person except for size has been a curse rather than a blessing. They have insisted on being accepted by society as normal persons. Yet if you are only two feet high, this is impossible. Frank Delphino, who, in addition to being a midget was also an extremely accomplished violinist, refused to give concerts if he was billed as a midget. As the impresarios well knew, the public was more interested in Delphino's stature than his musical ability, so they insisted on billing him as "the world's smallest violinist." Delphino resented this attitude so bitterly that finally he organized his own orchestra.

An especially unhappy case occurred in 1831, when a midget three feet three inches high married a very tall woman who was six feet six inches. Apparently, the midget felt that in making this match he was somehow compensating for his height and proving to the world that he could attract a big woman. Unfortunately, it was the little man's money and not his person that interested the woman. Soon after their marriage, she had an affair with a normal-sized man and, with an exquisite refinement of cruelty, used to put her miniature husband on the mantelpiece where he was forced to watch her amours with her lover—the midget afraid to jump off for fear of breaking his legs. Later, the woman's lover deserted her and she took poison. Seemingly, her little husband still loved her, for he drank the rest of the poison and

THE MIGHTY MIDGETS

they died together. This tragedy probably inspired Tod Browning's famous motion picture, *Freaks*, which has basically the same plot.

Such cases are rare. Although I have never experienced the ridicule and prejudice little people have to endure, I could never see why an individual should not take advantage of his height to earn a living any more than a fat, little Italian named Caruso should not have capitalized on his abnormal lung development or Mohammed Ali should not make money from the fact that he happens to have a punch like a pile driver. One is just as much a freak as the other.

It is easier to classify midgets than dwarfs because while there are many reasons for dwarfism, midgets are produced by only a few causes. This list of midget types was drawn up by Buddie Thompson who, in addition to being a pituitary midget himself, taught college biology for some years.

Mr Thompson divides all midgets into two groups: thyroid midgets and pituitary midgets. He believes that there are two types of thyroid midgets: the Mongoloids who have slanted eyes, are dull mentally and are usually the size of a three or four-year-old child with no sexual development; and the Cretins, who are slightly taller and slightly more intelligent but also do not develop sexually. An example of the Cretin midget was the "Aztec children" who toured Europe in the middle of the last century. They were both about thirty-four inches tall and virtual idiots. Advertised as members of a strange tribe living in the wilds of South America, they were actually the children of a couple living in San Salvador who sold them to a showman.

It is the pituitary midgets that one usually sees in shows. All pituitary midgets are normal at birth. Mr Thompson divides them into three classes. The infantile type number one is seldom taller than three and a half feet, more intelligent than a Cretin, but subnormal and listless with no sexual development. The infantile number two is taller, sometimes reaching a height of four feet, has normal intelligence (occasionally higher than normal) and sexual organs, but cannot have children. Lastly, there is the mature type, whose height is usually between three and a half feet and four feet. They have normal or superior intelligence and can function sexually. Mr Thompson puts himself in this group.

Being a midget is costly. All their clothes must be specially made (unless they are willing to wear children's clothes, which few midgets will do), and their shoes alone may cost a hundred dollars. If a midget drives a car, special costly mechanical adjustments have to be made. Food is also a problem. A midget eats as much as a normal-sized person, but cannot eat as much at one time. As one midget explained it to me, "We eat light but continuously." This creates a problem if a midget must often eat in restaurants, because he cannot finish a regular meal, but in two or three hours he will be hungry again. As a result of additional expenses, an ordinary job often will not pay enough for a midget to live on.

The midgets I have known seemed well adjusted. But others have emotional problems. High on midgets' hate list is being treated as children. Normal-sized people often do this instinctively; they offer to lift a midget into a chair, for example, or bring him a small-sized table to eat from. To most people this reaction may seem unreasonable, but then most people do not have to suffer the humiliations to which little people are occasionally subjected. Raymond Schultz, a midget who married a normal-sized woman and has normal children, came home one evening and was playing with the kids when a newly hired nurse came in and said briskly, "Well, to bed, children!" To Raymond's rage, he was ordered to bed with "the other children," and when he protested, the nurse threatened to spank him. He fired her the next morning.

Walter Bodin and Burnet Hersh in their now classical study of midgets, *It's a Small World* (Coward-McCann, 1934), say, "To survive decently in an overgrown world midgets must be egotists." Michael Dunn, the dwarf actor, admits to having a king-sized ego. "If I were not totally convinced I'm a superior person, I'd be a very inferior one," he once explained. I've never noticed this trait particularly, but it's proverbial that small men are inclined to be cocky. It has been said that if Napoleon had been five inches taller he never would have tried to conquer the world.

Virtually all midgets are born of normal parents, but a tendency to produce midgets does occur in some families. The Swensen family of Austin, Texas, have given birth to three generations of midgets. The Del Rios, with whom I worked on the Johnny J. Jones shows, are three midget children of the same parents. Paul is twenty-three inches tall and the two girls, Trinidad and Delores, two inches taller. When I knew them, Paul was twenty-two years old and the girls slightly older. They had several normal brothers and sisters who accepted them without any of the dislike some doctors claim children feel for a freakish sibling. Their sisters especially loved to dress up in the midgets' long evening gowns and strut around. One of the little girls split open the seams of a dinner dress and said accusingly to her midget sister, "You're growing smaller!" The midget good-naturedly replied, "No, darling, you're growing up." The child stared at her in astonishment. "You mean people get bigger?" she cried and burst into tears.

The Three Del Rios midgets: Trinidad, Paul and Delores.

I don't know if you'd say Paul was aggressive, but he certainly was fearless. I remember one night some drunks tried to break into the ten-in-one side show while Paul was playing a miniature piano as part of his act. He was a good musician and took his music seriously. Paul jumped off the catwalk, rushed at the drunks and tried to throw them out. They could easily have murdered him, but when they saw a little man two feet high wearing a dinner jacket coming for them, they let out a howl and ran.

I suppose that midgets, like most people who have been kicked around, enjoy turning the tables. Guy Patin, a French surgeon, says that in the seventeenth century, the empress of Austria had all the giants and midgets in the

Germanic empire assembled in Vienna for some kind of show she had in mind. They were all put in the same building, even though the officials were worried that the giants would ill-treat the midgets. It turned out the other way. The midgets delighted in teasing the giants and, being so small and quick, the giants could not catch them. At last, the poor giants had to beg the officials to protect them, and guards were put in the building to keep the midgets in their own quarters. It is not generally known that the famous (or notorious) Algonquin Round Table was founded by Robert Benchley and Dorothy Parker to protect Robert Sherwood from midgets. Mr Sherwood was six feet seven. (Once when Benchley was asked if he knew Sherwood, he jumped on a chair, held his hand as far up as possible and replied, "Know him? Why, I've known him since he was this high.") A troupe of midgets was playing at the Hippodrome near the Vanity Fair office where Sherwood, Benchley and Dorothy Parker worked, and whenever Sherwood left the building the midgets would follow him, asking, "How's the weather up there?" and other jibes. Finally, Parker and Benchley went along as guards for their giant friend and learned to rush him into the Algonquin for lunch. This was the origin of the Round Table.

Although Buddie Thompson does not feel that most of the characteristics researchers have ascribed to midgets are true, he admits that his people have their faults. A number of midgets become alcoholics. This is not surprising when you reflect that, other factors being equal, an individual's tolerance for liquor is in proportion to his body weight. An eighty-pound midget would be knocked on his ear by an amount of alcohol that would give an average-sized person a mild glow.

Rather surprisingly, some midget men have been notorious for their love affairs. In the last century, a midget caused a major scandal in the Viennese court by his behavior. Professor M. Truzzi in his paper on small people has suggested that midget men's success with normal women can more probably be attributed to the women's curiosity rather than to the little fellow's attractiveness, but perhaps Professor Truzzi is just jealous. Even though many midgets have been married successfully to normal-sized people, there are obviously problems which sometimes end quite tragically, other times happily.

Joseph Boruwlaski, usually called Count Boruwlaski, was a midget born in Russia in 1739. It is said that at the age of six he was only seventeen inches high, which, if true, would be very remarkable.*

He had a sister named Anastasia who was so much shorter that she could stand under his arm. Poor little Anastasia had a warm heart and fell in love with a dashing young officer. Knowing that he could never return her affection and also that he was desperately poor, she used to inveigle him into playing cards with her, always being careful to lose to provide her lover with an income. Unhappily, she died of smallpox at the age of twenty. Joseph, meanwhile, had been patronized by the Countess de Tarnow, who took him around with her on her travels through the courts of Europe. He made a great sensation, not only because of his size but also because of his quick wit. Once while he was sitting on the knee of Maria Theresa, her majesty asked him what was the most remarkable sight he had seen in his travels. "What I am seeing

---

* It is virtually impossible for a pituitary midget to be smaller than a new-born baby unless he is deformed [born without legs for example]; pituitary midgets are born normal, but later cease to grow. However, there are apparently exceptions to this rule as in the case of Lucia Zarate, whom I'll discuss later.

right now: such a little man in the lap of so great a lady," tactfully replied Joseph. The empress noticed he was looking intently at a ring on her finger and asked him what he thought of it. "I was not looking at the ring, but at your hand, which I beg permission to kiss," replied the little courtier. Maria Theresa was so pleased with this answer that she called over her daughter, Marie Antoinette, and taking a valuable diamond ring from her finger, gave it to Joseph. Later, the Princess Nassau-Weilbourg took the midget on her lap and asked him if he was not sorry to be so small. "Certainly not, for otherwise I would not have the honor to sit upon your ladyship's knee," replied Joseph. As a result of these little speeches, Joseph became quite a rich man.

When he was twenty-five, Joseph fell in love with an actress and sent her several expensive gifts. The woman pretended to reciprocate his devotion, but privately laughed at him among her friends. When the Countess de Tarnow heard of the affair, she angrily dropped Joseph, who was far more crushed by the action of his loved one than by the loss of the countess' patronage, for he was at once taken up by Stanislaus II, King of Poland. This experience discouraged Joseph from any more love affairs until he was forty, when he fell in love with a young woman named Isalina Barbutan. Isalina at first ridiculed the idea but when she learned the king approved of the match and was prepared to settle a hundred ducats on the couple, she changed her mind. The couple traveled widely and had several children. As far as I know, they were happy together.

Joseph's quick wit never deserted him. Once a fat woman asked him what his religion was. When he told her that he was a Roman Catholic, she angrily assured him he had no chance of going to heaven.

Eyeing the woman's bulk, Joseph retorted, "The Bible says that the gate to heaven is narrow, so I would suspect I have a better chance than you." Later, in England while staying at an inn, he happened to get into the room of Stephen Kemble, an actor so fat that he could play Falstaff without padding. The startled Kemble roughly demanded what he was doing there. "I'm going to exhibit myself at the fair tomorrow, and I suppose"—looking over Kemble's swollen body—"you're here for the same reason." Kemble was not amused.

Joseph was finally persuaded by the town council of Durham, England, to take up his permanent residence there in return for an annual annuity, the councilmen reasoning that the famous midget would make an outstanding tourist attraction. Tired of travel, Joseph consented and passed the rest of this life quietly in Durham. He died at the age of ninety-eight.

As long as the human race has existed, there must have been midgets and dwarfs. The first midget on record was Knoumtoptuwo—his name must have been longer than he was—who was chief steward of the linen to the pharaoh in 2,500 B.C. There were a number of famous midgets in antiquity, such as Philetas of Cos, a poet and philosopher, who lived around 330 B.C. and was tutor to Ptolemy Philadelphus. According to the story, Philetas was so small he had to wear lead shoes to keep from being blown away. Another learned midget was Alypius of Alexandria, who was said to have been seventeen inches tall. He was reputed to have been "a most excellent logician and philosopher . . . and scarce anything but spirit and soul." Alypius had too much spirit, for he quarreled with the ruler, Jamblicus, who had him imprisoned in a parrot's cage. In the Middle Ages midgets were highly esteemed, and in 1566 Cardinal Vitelli gave a banquet with thirty-four midget waiters. Peter the Great of Russia had a midget retainer named Valakoff who married the midget attendant of Princess Theodorovna. Peter gave them a great wedding with seventy-two midgets as guests.

Even in those days, it seems that midgets were high spirited and ready to stand up for themselves. Keysler, an eighteenth-century traveler in the Tyrol, tells of a midget at the court of the Archduke Ferdinand. One of the courtiers amused himself by poking fun at the little man, who was too small to defend himself. At last, the midget asked the archduke to drop his glove, which the surprised Ferdinand did. The trained courtier instantly bent over to pick it up, whereupon the midget kicked him in the face.

My own favorite historical midget was Jeffrey Hudson, who lived in the court of Charles I of England. Jeffrey was eighteen inches high. He was presented to the queen as a wedding gift, served to her in a large pie. When the queen cut the crust, the tiny man jumped out. Jeffrey was so small that he could masquerade as a cat. The Duchess of Buckingham had a pet feline of which she was very fond. Knowing this, some jokers at the court skinned the animal, covered Jeffrey with the skin and sent him, crawling on hands and knees, into the duchess' drawing room while she was giving a tea party. Jeffrey rubbed against the duchess' leg, mewing loudly, and the old lady without looking down broke off a piece of cake and asked, "Does Mother's precious want a goody?" "Hell no," replied Jeffrey, "pass me down some wine." The duchess fainted and the guests fled screaming. The duchess was accused of witchcraft, and finally Jeffrey had to

Prince Nicholi, the smallest man who ever lived. He was eighteen inches tall and weighed fifteen pounds. This photo was taken in 1871.

confess the prank. The noble jokers were banished from the court but, of course, nothing was done to the privileged midget.*

Jeffrey's greatest friend was the king's giant porter, William Evans, who used to carry the midget around in his pocket. He saved Jeffrey's life when the little man was nearly blown into the Thames during a high wind, but Jeffrey could look out after

---

* Buddie Thompson assures me this is impossible; no midget could be small enough to pass for a cat. Well, it's a good story anyhow.

himself. Once he was attacked by a big turkey cock and forced to defend himself with his little sword. It was a terrific struggle, but Jeffrey finally won and ate the loser.

In 1640, Jeffrey was sent to France as a secret agent for the king. As a freak, Jeffrey was able to operate with a freedom impossible to a normal man. He carried out his mission and was returning to England when his ship was captured by Dutch privateers. Jeffrey was able to save the confidential papers he was carrying and delivered them safely to the king, who knighted him as a reward.

This was a time of trouble in England; it was during a long drawn-out civil war. Charles's queen fled back to her native France, and in 1649 Charles was executed. Sir Jeffrey, however, considered an irresponsible freak by the king's conquerors, escaped injury.

In 1653, he slipped off to France to join the exiled queen's court. Another courtier named Robert Crofts laughed at the midget and Jeffrey challenged the man to a duel. The midget came to the field of honor riding a pony so that he and his opponent would be the same height. Crofts, who did not take the business seriously, turned up carrying no weapons except a squirt gun. This made Jeffrey furious. He said coldly, "Very good, sir. As that is the weapon you have selected, defend yourself." He raised his own pistol and shot Crofts dead.

Even for the privileged midget, deliberately killing an unarmed man was considered going too far. Jeffrey was expelled from the court. He felt he had been unfairly treated and took to the sea. There he was captured by Barbary corsairs and sold as a slave in Algiers. For the next few years he led a miserable life until he could be ransomed. Even then he was in no for-

giving mood and spent his time plotting revenge against the court. In 1679, he took part in the so-called "Popish Plot." As a result, Sir Jeffrey was imprisoned. He was released in 1682 at the age of sixty-three, but died shortly afterwards.

Almost equaling Jeffrey in deeds of derring-do was Richebourg, who was a sort of pint-sized Scarlet Pimpernel. He was only twenty-three inches high and in the service of the Duchess of Orleans. During the French Revolution, Richebourg was disguised as a baby and taken into Paris with letters hidden in his diaper. He was also able to smuggle letters out in the same way. When the opportunity arose, his "nurse" would put him down and the midget would scamper off to deliver his messages. If anyone came along, Richebourg would sit down, cooing and waving his little hands until the danger was passed. After the Revolution, the Orleans family retired him on a pension. He had so many enemies that he never left the house for the last twenty-four years of his life. He lived to be ninety.

Unquestionably, the most famous midget in history was General Tom Thumb, born Charles Sherwood Stratton but rechristened by P.T. Barnum, probably the greatest showman of all time. Charles Stratton was born in 1832 in Bridgeport, Connecticut, of normal parents who had several other children. He weighed nine pounds at birth, but at the age of six months stopped growing. He was then slightly under two feet. His parents were ashamed of him and kept the child a virtual prisoner in the house until he was ten years old, but rumors of the tiny boy got around. When Barnum went to Bridgeport to visit his brother, he heard of the boy. He offered the family three dollars a week for the boy and they were glad to get rid of him. Barnum was to make millions from the midget.

After changing his name, Barnum dressed him in adult clothing to make him look older and taught him a few simple songs and dances. He took the boy to England, where he created a sensation. He gave a command performance for Queen Victoria in Buckingham Palace and delighted everyone. When the time came to retire, Barnum, in accordance with protocol, walked backwards and Tom tried to do the same, but finding himself unable to keep up, turned and ran a few steps and then solemnly turned again and walked backwards, keeping this up until he reached the door, to the great delight of the court. The queen had a special coach made for him three and a half feet tall by four feet long with a team of miniature horses. (The carriage is now in the Circus Hall of Fame in Sarasota, Florida.) So popular was Tom that when Haydon, the great artist, gave an exhibition of his paintings, no one came. The crowds were all going to see Tom Thumb. Haydon killed himself, leaving a note saying that Tom Thumb had murdered him.

Barnum next took Tom on a tour of the continent which was equally successful. Tom Thumb dolls were created, Tom Thumb gingerbread men sold and a Tom Thumb restaurant opened in Paris. Tom himself was no fool and he insisted on a share of the profits. When he returned to America, Tom was a rich man and able to retire at twenty. He bought an estate near Bridgeport, got a yacht, a stable of thoroughbreds and indulged his taste for jewelry.

A few years later, due to some unfortunate speculations, Barnum went bankrupt. Tom Thumb good-naturedly came out of retirement to help his old friend. Meanwhile, Barnum had acquired three other midgets: "Commodore" George Nutt, and Lavinia and Minnie Warren, midget sisters.

All three were smaller than Tom, who now at thirty had shot up to three feet, but his name was still magic. Such crowds came to see him that Barnum was able to pay off his debts and Tom, incidentally, made another fortune for himself.

Tom fell in love with Lavinia Warren on sight. As he told Barnum, "Mr Barnum, that is the most charming little lady I ever saw and I believe she was made on purpose to be my wife." But Tom discovered he had a rival in Commodore Nutt, who was so jealous that he attacked Tom and beat him up in a dressing room. Tom, it seems, was afraid of the determined little commodore and retired to Bridgeport, but secretly arranged with Barnum to bring Lavinia up to visit him. When the Commodore heard of the plot, he took the next train to Bridgeport himself, vowing vengeance against Tom, but he arrived too late. Tom and Lavinia were engaged. Later, the Commodore got over his anger and agreed to be Tom's best man.

The wedding, held in Grace Church in New York in 1863, was such a sensation that police reserves had to be called out to handle the crowds. The most prominent people in the city fought for invitations, and the church was so packed that scores of people fainted. Later, the couple went to Washington, where they were received by President Lincoln and then toured Europe, where Tom made a third fortune. It is said that Lavinia had a baby, but I have also heard that this was a publicity stunt of Barnum's. If true, the child did not live.

The couple lived in luxury in Bridgeport until 1883, when Tom died. After his death, Lavinia discovered that her free-spending husband had managed to run through his considerable wealth and there was nothing left. She married an Italian midget named Count Primo Magri. They went on tour, but without Barnum's genius at securing publicity, the tour was a failure. Poor little Lavinia became less and less of an attraction until she died in a Coney Island side show at the age of seventy-eight.

Who was the smallest person to ever live? This question has been asked millions of times and there is no real answer. Every midget is billed as the "smallest person in the world" so, to avoid contradiction, they refuse to allow themselves to be measured (as do giants).*

Also, since a midget generally continues to grow, if only slightly (in addition to the sudden increase of height most experience at thirty), it makes a great deal of difference whether the midget is measured at the age of ten or twenty. *The Guinness Book of World Records* listed the shortest adult human as Pauline Musters, a Dutch midget, who died in 1895. She was then exactly two feet. *Life* once published a life-sized picture of a midget. It took two pages and even then the magazine had to cheat a little on the margins. That would make the midget about twenty-two inches high. I believe he was about twenty years old.

I have always believed that Lucia Zarate, born in Mexico in 1864, was the smallest person who ever lived. Apparently, *The Guinness Book of World Records* did not accept her because she was never measured by doctors as was Pauline Musters (after death). She was said to have been seven inches when she was born, and never grew to be more than twenty inches. I have seen pictures of her and she was certainly minute; I should say well under two feet and supposedly weighing only five pounds. As she was gentle, charming and intelligent everyone who knew her seems to have liked her. Sadly, poor Lucia died, in 1890, while on tour. The

train she was aboard stalled in a blizzard near Truckee, California, and she succumbed to the cold.

Lucia Zarate was the smallest woman who ever lived. Her height has been recorded as both seventeen and twenty inches tall. Reportedly she weighed only five pounds. She died on 1890 when the circus train in which she was traveling was stalled by a blizzard in the Sierra Nevada Mountains.

---

* About the only way you ever get to measure a giant is after he's dead, which has led to some gruesome episodes as I'll explain in the next chapter.

4 The Gentle Giants

Little people may have problems, but their problems are nothing compared to the difficulties of giants. Giants have all the troubles of the little people: their clothing must be specially made; they can drive only custom-designed cars; beds, chairs and tables are not adapted to them; and, in addition, they cannot ride in trains, planes or buses because they do not fit into the seats. Also, extremely tall giants are apt to be sickly, unlike midgets and dwarfs, who are usually tough little characters.

Normal men have always regarded giants with a mixture of awe and fear. Most men would like to be taller and stronger than they are, so they may look on giants with some envy. But historically, giants have had bad press—one seldom reads legends about a good giant. Both in Greek and Norse mythology, giants are represented as enemies of the gods, creatures who had to be overthrown before the gods could take their rightful places. Giants are always described as enormously strong but stupid and clumsy. They are easily outwitted by a clever man like Jack the Giant Killer. (The origin of Jack was the Norse god Jalk, noted for his exploits against the great Jotums.) There is no biological reason why a giant should not have normal intelligence, and several giants have been brilliant men. However, the fact that it is difficult for them to get around may tend to make some appear stupid.

How tall do you have to be in order to be considered a giant? There is no fixed height, but Polly Jae Lee in her excellent book, *Giant*, considers that anyone fifteen inches taller than the average man can be called a giant, pointing out that to a Pygmy a six-foot man would be a giant while among the tall Watusi, a seven-foot man would be only slightly taller than the average. In our society, I'd say anyone over

Chang Yu Sang, born in Peking, 1847, was more than 8 feet tall.

seven and a half feet would be considered a giant.

As with midgets, most giants are the result of malfunctioning of the pituitary gland. In giants, the gland overacts instead of underacting. Again as with midgets, the majority of giants are normal at birth and it is not until they are several years old that they begin to shoot up, usually to their own horror as well as the horror of their families. If they reach maturity before the glands go haywire, they do not increase in height, but their hands and feet enlarge. This condition is called acromegaly and the giant, like the dwarf, becomes deformed. Otherwise, although tall, he is symmetrically proportioned, but may well have extra long legs. Legs are usually a giant's weak point. Not only are they naturally spindly, but they must support the great weight of his body, which often runs to 450 or 500 pounds—even if the man is not fat. Some giants have only been able to walk by putting their hands on the shoulders of two normal men. But by no means are all giants cripples. Many have been perfectly able-bodied and some have been capable of feats of such strength that they rival the exploits of the giants in fairy tales.

Undoubtedly, the most famous giant in history was Goliath, the Philistine champion who was defeated by David, the shepherd boy. Goliath was not a Philistine but a Rephaim, one of a race of exceptionally tall people whom the Israelites had previously defeated. The Bible says he was "six cubits and a span." As we don't know exactly the length of the Biblical cubit, Goliath's exact height is uncertain, but he was around ten feet tall. His coat of mail weighed five thousand shekels of brass (156 pounds) and his spear (actually a javelin intended for throwing) weighed six hundred shekels of iron (nineteen pounds). In II Samuel 21:20, the Bible goes on to tell

of four giants, apparently Goliath's brothers, one of whom had six fingers on each hand and six toes on each foot. Curiously, at the close of the last century, a French doctor De Cyon described a family of giants who all had six toes. De Cyon also says they suffered from headaches and eye trouble, and were mentally retarded.

Just as people have always been fascinated by the idea of a land inhabited by tiny Pygmies, so they have told stories of countries inhabited by giants. While making his famous voyage around the southern tip of South America, Magellan thought he had discovered such a place. The Indians he met there seemed to him enormous and he named them Patagonians because he considered their height to be five cubits, or seven and a half feet. From then on, every explorer seems to have encountered these giant Indians and they got bigger and bigger until Sebald de Weert, a Dutch captain, said (in 1598) they were twelve feet tall. Then they started shrinking. In 1785, some Spanish officers measured a number of Patagonians and said they averaged six feet and a half with a few seven feet, about the size of the modern Watusi in Africa. In 1849, a Captain Bourne who lived in Patagonia confirms this. If this giant race really did exist, they have now disappeared and no trace of them has ever been found.

For centuries, men have taken for granted that all giants were terrifically strong. This would seem reasonable. All other factors being equal, a heavyweight can beat a welterweight and a welterweight is stronger than a lightweight. So a giant should be far stronger than an ordinary man. Then it was found that giants are often quite weak due to their special physical conformation. Soon the statement was being made, even in medical textbooks, that all giants are weaklings. Perhaps this made ordinary people feel better, but it plainly isn't true. Some giants have been very strong.

One of the first giants we know anything about was Maximinus, who was emperor of Rome from 235 to 238 A.D. According to accounts, Maximinus was between eight and nine feet tall. He started out in life as a Thracian shepherd, and when the Roman legions marched through Thrace, he was so intrigued by them that he offered himself as a legionnaire. The general doubted that anyone so big could handle himself well and, calling out the two strongest men in the legion, told Maximinus to pick one and wrestle him. The giant replied that he'd wrestle both together. It was no contest. The giant picked up both men, one under each arm, and, while they kicked and struggled like children, carried them over to the general and dumped them at his feet. Naturally, the general was impressed, but even so decided that Maximinus was too gigantic to fit in the legions. Maximinus, however, was as stubborn as he was big. He followed the general the next day when the legion broke camp. Annoyed, the general cantered his horse for a mile or so to lose the giant, but when he drew rein, there was Maximinus running easily alongside him. After that, the general took him on.

Maximinus is said to have been able to use his wife's bracelet as a ring, eat forty pounds of meat a day, and drink six gallons of wine. Once on a wager he pulled a loaded cart that two oxen had been unable to move. He was a good soldier and rose in the ranks until he became a general. When the weak Emperor Alexander was murdered in a conspiracy, the legions elected Maximinus emperor. Maximinus was reluctant to accept the honor, but was finally persuaded to don the purple.

Understandably, the unlettered giant made a far better soldier than he did an emperor. He disliked both Rome and the Roman politicians and showed it. He avoided the capital and spent all his time leading his troops in battles against the German tribes. At last, his general staff, probably bribed by the politicians, decided to murder him. Maximinus knew of the conspiracy and he sent his young son away. When the conspirators burst into his tent, they found him waiting for them, sword in hand. None of them dared to face the giant (it is said that in one engagement eight men attacked him and Maximinus killed all of them single-handedly), but one of them shoved the body of his son toward him on the end of a spear. At that sight, all the fight went out of the giant. Sinking to his knees, he sobbed, "You might have spared the boy; he never hurt you." Then the assassins closed in and butchered the unresisting man.

Another giant of amazing strength was William Joyce, who gave an exhibition before King William of England in 1699. He lifted a one-ton weight, then tied one end of a rope around his waist and the other to "an extraordinarily strong horse" which even when whipped was unable to budge him. He concluded by breaking the rope, which was "of incredible thickness," with his bare hands and then pulling up a tree a yard and a half in circumference by the roots. Unfortunately, we don't know his height, only that he was of "gigantic stature."

In modern times, there was Angus McAskill, a Scottish giant who exhibited himself in Barnum's American Museum. McAskill was seven feet nine inches and weighed 405 pounds. He used to hold a platter while Tom Thumb did a clog dance on it. McAskill could easily lift a weight of fifteen hundred pounds. Once a smart aleck in the audience, who had heard that giants were really weak and thought McAskill's act was a fake, challenged him to a boxing match. McAskill tried to pass the matter off as a joke, but when the man became abusive, agreed to the bout if the challenger would first shake hands to show there were no hard feelings. The man consented and McAskill gave him such a grip his hand was crushed. He decided against the fight. For a thousand-dollar wager, McAskill once lifted an anchor weighing 2,200 pounds, but this was a little too much for him. He strained himself and never completely recovered. He finally retired to Nova Scotia with his fame and wealth.

A giant who was not only enormously strong but also possessed quite a sense of humor was Anthony Payne, born in Cornwall during the sixteenth century. Payne's humor was rather bloodthirsty, as befitted a giant, but usually he was most good-natured. He was born in the manor house of Stratton, the property of Sir Beville Granville, and, when he grew up, became the devoted servant of Sir Beville's eldest son, John. Anthony's height was seven feet four inches. At feasts, he would carry in the carcass of a red deer (weighing about 350 pounds) to be roasted in the fireplace. Once when a boy and a donkey were lost in the forest while gathering wood, Anthony carried the donkey plus the load of wood back on his shoulder.

Anthony followed his master in the war against Cromwell and once after a bloody battle was given the task of burying ten of the dead. The giant dug a trench long enough to hold ten corpses, put in nine bodies, and was carrying off the tenth when the supposed corpse cried out, "Surely you wouldn't bury me before I'm dead?"

Payne was surprised, but he retorted glibly enough. "I tell thee, man, the trench was dug for ten and there's nine in it already; you must take your place."

"But I bean't dead, I say. I haven't done living yet. Be massyful—don't ye hurry a poor fellow into the earth before his time."

"I won't hurry thee; I mean to put thee down quietly and cover thee up, and then thee cans't die at thy leisure."

This conversation put the other gravediggers into stitches. What the wounded man thought isn't on record. Anthony finally relented and carried the injured man to his own home.

After the beheading of Charles I, a Tory officer had a calf's head served up on a plate to ridicule the dead king. Anthony was furious and hurled both head and plate out the window. Angry words followed and a duel was arranged. The giant easily beat down his opponent's guard and then ran him through the shoulder, shouting as the blood spurted out, "There's some sauce to go with your calf's head!"

Sir Beville Granville was killed at the battle of Lansdowne with Anthony fighting at his side, his sword "going like the arm of a windmill" as one observer reported. At the death of their leader, the troops broke, but Anthony picked up John Granville, then sixteen, put him on his father's horse and shouted to the men to come back. They did and won.

Charles II made Anthony a yeoman of the guard, but when John Granville was appointed governor of Plymouth, Anthony insisted on going with him. He was given the post of halberdier of the guns. His portrait, painted by Sir Godfrey Kneller, shows him leaning on a cannon while his wine flask, which held a full gallon, lay beside him.

Unlike many giants, Anthony lived to a ripe old age and died at Stratton. His body was so huge it could not be carried down the stairs, so a hole was cut in the floor and he was lowered by ropes to the ground.

Not all giants have been heroes. Some have led tragic lives. One of the most pitiful was Charles Byrne, the Irish giant who lived in the latter part of the eighteenth century. We know exactly how tall he was: he stood seven feet nine inches, although he claimed to be eight feet two inches. Charles was the son of Irish peasants and he allowed himself to be exhibited until he had saved up enough to retire. He changed all his savings into a single seven-hundred-pound note. Unhappily, Charles was fond of the bottle and got drunk that night. Thieves stole his bank note.

This was a double disaster for poor Charles because he was always surrounded by a horde of doctors waiting for him to die so they could get his skeleton. The most persistent was Dr John Hunter, who even took to following the giant around with a large iron pot to boil the giant's flesh off his bones. The sight of the doctor's pot was too much for Charles's nerves; he started desperately to exhibit himself, saving every penny to be assured of a safe burial. He overdid it and died of a nervous breakdown, first making a group of friends swear to protect his corpse.

So determined were the doctors that one even bribed the undertaker to make a trap door in the side of the coffin so he could steal the body after the funeral ceremony. But it was John Hunter who finally obtained the huge corpse. He had agents ply Charles's friends with whiskey until they passed out. Then he removed the corpse and filled the coffin with rocks; Charles went into the black kettle. What is left of his skeleton is now at the Royal College of Surgeons in London.

Hunter was so determined to secure Charles's body because he hoped to find the reason for his abnormal growth. He

never did and it was not until 1915 that Dr Walter M. Kraus, while studying the skull of a midget, noticed the tiny hole where the pituitary gland had been located and rightly concluded that it was this gland that influences growth.

Few giants have been good showmen; usually they just stand still and let people look at them. An exception was Patrick Cot-

"Lofty," whose real name is Jan Van Albert, was from Holland and stood 8 feet 6½ inches tall. His cigar is being lit by Fred "Pip" Aslett, a well-known London midget who was 28 inches tall. Prior to World War II they toured the world with a show called "Would You Believe It?"

ter, another Irish giant. Patrick took the name of O'Brien to capitalize on Charles Byrne's fame—a doubtful compliment under the circumstances. As a seventeen-year-old boy, Patrick was so tall that a showman offered his father fifty pounds a year to exhibit the eight-foot-seven-inch youngster. The father accepted, but soon Patrick refused to allow himself to be exhibited without receiving any of the gate. As a result, the showman had him imprisoned for debt. A benevolent gentleman bailed Patrick out and the boy went into show business for himself in London theaters in 1785. In the first three days, Patrick made thirty pounds, at that time a considerable sum of money. His career was launched.

Patrick thought of several devices for publicizing himself. At Sadler's Wells he walked around the stalls and shook hands with people in the boxes. When walking down the street, he would casually take the covers off street lamps and light his pipe by the flame. It was the custom for women to sit by open second-floor windows to watch people pass and get a breeze. Patrick used to lean in the windows and kiss them, which must have given the ladies quite a surprise. He also circulated the story that once while riding in his specially made carriage, a highwayman stopped it. When Patrick stepped out, the highwayman fled in terror.

Warned by the fate of poor Charles, Patrick carefully saved his money and retired a wealthy man. He had his tomb carved twelve feet deep out of rock and left instructions that after he was buried, the grave was to be covered with iron bars set in bricks. He also made sure that his pallbearers would be teetotalers. His plans were successful and the doctors never got Patrick.

Probably the tallest man in the world today is Johann K. Petursson, the "Icelandic Giant," who is billed as being eight feet eight inches tall, although it must be remembered that traditionally in their publicity giants add a few inches to their height. He came to this country in 1948 and exhibited himself in side shows for two hundred a week. His price soon went up to five hundred and then, instead of working in side shows, Petursson took to exhibiting himself in his own show as the only attraction (this is called a single O). Only a very outstanding freak can do this, and, of course, the profits are much greater. Petursson is probably the highest-paid freak in show business today. In addition to his entrance fee, he sells his finger rings, which are almost big enough to be a bracelet for an ordinary man. He probably nets well over a thousand dollars a week. Like Patrick O'Brien, Petursson is an excellent showman. He works in Viking costume with an ornate headdress that makes him look even bigger than he is, and has grown a long beard which makes him more impressive. Petursson lives is Gibsonton, Florida, is now semi-retired and still goes on the road occasionally although he has no need of money. He simply enjoys the life.

Occasionally, as do midgets, giants marry each other. The best known giant couple are Mr and Mrs Fred Fisher, who have now retired from show business and own a motel near Sarasota, Florida. Mr Fisher was born in Vienna, Austria, and his wife comes from Bernstadt, Germany. He is billed as being eight feet one inch tall and weighing 240 pounds. She is seven feet eleven inches and weighs 209. Unlike most giants, the Fisher's height is not the result of a pituitary problem. They are simply big people and come from families of very large people. Whereas many pituitary giants have abnormally long legs, the Fishers are perfectly proportioned.

I have known only one giant myself. He was Al Tomaini, who was billed as being eight feet four inches. Al was married to Jeanie, the "half woman" (she was born without legs). Anyone who thinks giants are stupid should have known Al. He was not only a good showman but an excellent businessman. He and Jeanie, after appearing for some years in side shows as (naturally) the "World's Strangest Married Couple," opened their own show, which was notably successful.

Al is dead now, but Jeanie is very much alive and lives in Gibsonton, Florida, where I had the chance to renew our old acquaintance. I should say something about this unique community. Gibsonton is a small town some fourteen miles south of Tampa on Route 41. The area was formerly owned by a J.B. Gibson, but its history really began in 1924, when Eddie LeMay, who used to run the cookhouse concession with a carnival, moved there and put up a restaurant called Eddie's Hut. Gibsonton is a pleasant spot on the Alafia River, with some of the most magnificent live oaks I have ever seen. It soon became winter quarters for carnies and, undoubtedly, has more freaks per square mile than any other spot in the world. In the spring when the carnies go on the road, the town empties out and doesn't refill until after Thanksgiving. It has the finest showman's clubhouse in America—the International Independent Showmen's Association of Gibsonton—as well as a retirement village for show people whose traveling days are over.

In 1949, Jeanie and Al retired from show business, moved to Gibsonton and built the Giant's Cafe, which has a huge billboard showing Al in the cowboy costume he always wore and one of his gigantic boots mounted on a pedestal. Jeanie lives in a pleasant house with a swimming pool and an aviary (one of her two adopted daughters is a bird lover). Jeanie had not changed much since I first met her in the '40s, although she said regretfully that she had put on some weight. "You remember my acrobatic act," she said as she led the way into her cool living room, walking easily on her hands. "I used to do somersaults, stand on one hand, and things like that. I haven't kept it up, so I'm not as slender as I was thirty years ago." Going over to a sofa, Jeanie swung herself up on

The "World's Strangest Married Couple," Jeanie (the "Only Living Half-Girl") and Giant Al Tomaini, height 8 feet 4½ inches. They were married September 28, 1936 in Ripley, New York, and lived in Florida.

it with a single flip of her body as easily as the average person would sit down. To realize what this means, try kneeling by a sofa and throwing yourself up on it, landing in a sitting position—and Jeanie was not on her knees but resting on her trunk.

Jeanie still runs the cafe, a tourist court and a boat yard where fishermen can rent boats for a day on the Alafia. "It keeps me pretty busy," she admitted. "When Al was alive, he used to drive me everywhere, but after his death I had to learn to drive myself. I have a special car with automatic shift and a hand-controlled brake. That car has made me lazy; I use it instead of exercising as I should."

The giants, Al Tomaini and Jack Earl (in cowboy shirt) pose with a normal-sized man in September, 1937.

Jeanie and Al met at the Dodson World Fair Shows in April, 1936. They were married that September. In 1941, they opened their own side show with the James Strates Shows. "We had Wally White, the human pincushion; Bill Cass, the anatomical wonder; and some other acts," she recalls. "Al built the bannerline [the string of gaudily painted canvas drawings that advertise the attractions inside], most of our props and the platforms. He was always good with his hands and had powerful arms and shoulders. His only problem was with his feet. They would trouble him if he stood too long." Al was a pituitary giant and nearly all such giants have trouble with their feet. Al weighed 350 pounds, although he was far from fat. This great weight plus the weakened leg bones is sure to cause complications.

Al was born in New Jersey in 1918, one of a family of seven, all normal except for himself. He was a normal-sized boy, but soon after ten years of age he began to shoot up. By the time he was twelve, he was six feet two inches tall. His parents took him to a doctor who was able to slow his growth somewhat, which probably explains why he was always comparatively healthy. After adopting the two little girls, the Tomainis decided to leave show business because they felt the constant traveling would be too hard on the children. So they opened the Giant's Cafe, which was an immediate success.

"Both on the road and here, I always did all the housework," Jeanie assured me. "I'm a good cook and I manage to get around about as easily as a normal person. Cooking for Al was no problem. You hear stories of giants eating half a sheep at a sitting and so on, but Al had no more appetite than a normal, active man." I have talked to several side-show impresarios who tell me that there seems to be no general rule about giants' eating habits; some eat a great deal, others little more than the average man.

Jeanie herself comes from Indiana. She has eight brothers and sisters, all normal. She had a happy childhood and got on well in school. Then her mother died and the family moved to Fort Wayne. Trying to help the child, her father put her in a home for cripples. Jeanie hated it. Since the teachers took for granted that none of the students would ever be outside of an institution, the school there was very bad. Jeanie left shortly and studied at home. Later, she went into show business where she met Al.

I asked Jeanie how her husband had felt about being a giant. "When people asked him, he always told them: 'Well, it's a living.' Actually, it was a nuisance trying to be comfortable in a world made for smaller people. He had to sleep in an extra-large, specially made bed. His shoes had to be specially made on a special last and cost fifty dollars—this was when you could get a good pair of shoes for six dollars. All his clothing had to be specially made. Al accepted all the inconveniences philosophically. He was born like that and didn't complain.

"I've had a good life," Jeanie concluded. "I've traveled, met lots of interesting people, and Al and I had a happy marriage. Financially, we did better than most people, and there is very little the average person can do that I can't. Al organized the first fire department this town ever had and was active in politics. I don't do much in that line myself. Running the cafe, boathouse and motel keeps me too busy."

I've said that I knew only one giant. Technically, that is true, but I had a friend who, although only about six feet eight, had all the characteristics generally associated with giants. His name was Corny; he weighed over three hundred pounds and was phenomenally strong. He had several brothers, all equally proportioned. When I met his mother, she glanced at me and remarked, "Your voice is so deep over the phone I didn't think you'd turn out to be a little fellow." Since I am six feet four and weigh 230 pounds, I've never forgotten that. Corny and I shared an interest in ornithology. One afternoon we were on a bird-watching expedition in the New Jersey swamps, Corny driving ahead in his old station wagon while the rest of us followed in my car. It was winter and bitterly cold, although not quite freezing. A drainage ditch some twenty feet wide ran parallel to the road, and beside the ditch we came on a parked car with a game warden standing beside it. Near him was a snowy owl which he had just wounded. In those days snowy owls were not protected.

Corny stopped the car and, getting out, began telling the warden what he thought of him for shooting a rare and beautiful bird. Corny never swore and never used an obscene word, but he had an Irish tongue and could express himself well without profanity. The angry warden retorted in kind. Suddenly, Corny grabbed the man and threw him right over the top of his car far out into the ditch. Then Corny collected the owl and drove on. The warden came crawling out of the ditch with his gun in his hand, swearing he was going to shoot Corny, but he was in no shape to do anything except get home as fast as he could.

On another bird-watching trip, we stopped after dark in a little bar and grill to warm ourselves; it had been raining and we were all soaked. There was a blazing fire burning in an open fireplace and a few patrons were sitting around at tables, including two effeminate young men sipping sherry and holding hands. Corny walked over to the fire and, as casually as if he were in his own home, peeled off his clothes and stood in his red woollen underwear, warming his ample behind at the blaze. No one, including the proprietor, said anything, but the two young men burst into titters and muttered, "My dear, did you ever? I really can't bear it, darling." Corny ignored them for some time and then, strolling over to them, brought his fist—which was roughly the size of a ten-pound ham—down on the table. He did not seem to strike hard, but the table cracked clean across.

"Well, girls, tell me what the joke is so we can all laugh together," boomed Corny in his great voice. The two men sat literally paralyzed with terror until Corny turned and went back to the fire. Then they fled the room. The owner was as awed as they were, for he never even asked us to pay for the table.

Corny once was able to do me a good turn. My wife and I had just returned to Philadelphia in the middle of winter from a prolonged stay in Africa. We picked up the children and were driving through Fairmount Park when I failed to come to a complete halt at a stop sign. A young policeman materialized out of nowhere and demanded to see my license. I produced it, but it had expired.

"You can't drive this car without a license," the officer bellowed at me.

I explained the circumstances and produced my passport. "That don't mean nothing to me," he roared. "Don't try to drive that car away from here."

"Surely you don't mean for me to sit all night in zero weather in the middle of Fairmount Park in an unheated car with two small children," I protested.

"Look, mister, I don't make the laws; I only enforce them," he shouted.

At this moment, who of all people happened to drive up but Corny. He stopped the car and asked, "Having trouble, Dan?"

When I told him what had happened, Corny got out of the car and walked over to the young officer who visibly quailed as Corny towered over him.

"What's all this about my friend not being able to drive his car?" said Corny in a voice that sounded like Vesuvius getting ready to erupt.

"I'm only trying to do my job," whined the policeman.

"I'm driving out of here and he's coming with me," boomed Corny. "Got it?"

"Sure, sure, if you're going to be with him, that's fine with me," whimpered the formerly tough cop. "I don't want to make no trouble."

We drove off together. I regret to say that Corny is dead now. We shall not look upon his like again.

Who was the tallest man who ever lived? There is considerable doubt about who was the smallest person, but we can be pretty sure who was the tallest, at least in medical history. He was Robert Wadlow, born in Alton, Illinois, in 1918. Robert died when he was in his early twenties and measured eight feet eleven point one inches, just a shade under nine feet. Robert is the only giant I ever heard of who didn't mind being measured, mainly because he was so darned tall that there was no question that he was the world's tallest human.

Robert was a normal baby, but soon began to grow. When he was nine, he could pick up his father like a doll. Robert was one freak who was definitely not happy with his abnormal condition. His father was an engineer and Robert hoped to be a lawyer. Although he had an excellent mind, he soon realized this was impossible. His huge fingers could not hold an ordinary pencil or pen, nor could he sit in an ordinary chair. As he increased in height, his legs could not bear the weight of his great frame. Although he was painfully thin, he weighed nearly 450 pounds. Even the most good-natured kidding hurt his feelings and often he would burst into tears, sobbing, "It's not my fault I am like this." He was forced to exhibit himself with Ringling Brothers, even though he had to wear a brace on his leg to support his weight. In 1940, the brace rubbed a sore on his leg that got infected. He died a few days later.

Jeanie, the "half woman," seen doing her acrobatic act with the Johnny J. Jones Shows in 1942. She was born August 23, 1918 in Indiana, the sixth child of nine, "born with no sign or semblance of lower limbs. Despite this so-called handicap, I am able to do almost anything any other girl can do, and was able to complete my education before entering show business."

5

Look Ma, Three Hands!

Today, few freak shows are left—in fact, only four real ones that feature several freaks: the Whitey Sutton side show with the James Strates Shows, featuring Percilla and Emmett and Bill Durkus, the three-eyed man; the Walter Wanous side show with Godding Amusements; Norman Brooks with Century 21 Shows; and the

Margarete Clark, with the James Strates Shows in 1949. She has a Siamese twin appendage growing out of her belly.

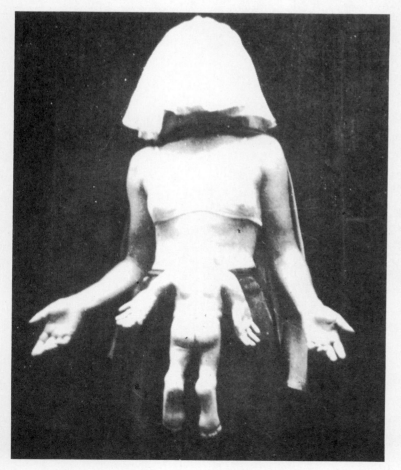

Ward Hall Show, now with Goodings' Million Dollar Midway.

Because certain "reformers" have been so outspoken in their attacks on freak shows as being "degrading," I have wondered if the public's interest in freaks has been waning. Ward Hall (who left home at the age of thirteen to join a circus and opened his own side show in 1948) assures me that freaks are more popular than ever. The trouble is, he says, that there aren't enough freaks. "Back in the '40s, there were so many carnivals and circuses that they played every small town. If there was a freak in the community, he'd go to the side show and ask to join. His family was probably ashamed of him, he had no friends and no employer would hire him. To be with people who regarded his deformity as an asset meant everything to him. Also, in those days circus life seemed glamorous to most people whether they were freaks or not. Now there are only a few shows left and they play mostly the big cities. If a child is a freak, he's put in an institution. Also, circus life isn't as romantic as it used to be."

Joseph Hilton, who ran side shows for many years and now operates a peep show with pictures of famous freaks, agrees. "There's nothing so fascinates most people as freaks, but there are only a few around. If they can't be taught a trade, they're put in an institution."

Nate Eagle, who was famous for his midget villages, summed up the situation by saying, ". . . all [freaks are] in institutions now." T.W. Kelly, another old-time showman, had an even grimmer suggestion: "I don't believe the doctors let them live. If a deformed baby is born and the doctor sees he's incurable, they think they're doing the parents and the child a favor by seeing that the infant quietly dies."

Some legislative bodies consider that they are improving public morals by banning freak shows. In 1969, when World Fair Shows opened in North Bay Village, Florida, the freaks were forbidden to appear, the prohibition being based on a 1921 state law that classed them with pornography. Ward Hall fought the law up to the state supreme court, the suit being filed in the name of Sealo (a famous old performer who has no arms, his hands growing directly from his shoulders and resembling the flippers of a seal) and little Pete Terhune, the versatile dwarf. By a six-to-one decision, the court directed that "one who is handicapped must be allowed a reasonable chance to earn a living." However, the feeling that there is something inherently wrong with exhibiting freaks is widespread. In England, a man was arrested for exhibiting a two-headed calf.

These well-meaning people do not realize that to condemn freaks to a life in an institution is to make them vegetables. In show business they can meet other people who are also freaks (often marrying), make a good income, travel, and be independent. Many freaks cannot perform any tasks. This is especially true of double-bodied people such as Siamese twins.

An especially tragic example of the unintentional cruelty exhibited by reformers is the case of poor little Rita-Christina, who was born in 1829 in Sassari, Sardinia, of desperately poor parents. The child—or children—had a double body above the waist. As a result, Rita-Christina had two heads, four arms, four lungs, two hearts, two stomachs, but only one bladder and two legs. The heads slept at different times and had completely different dispositions. Rita was inclined to be sad, while Christina was happy and gay. Unable to care for the baby properly, the parents exhibited her. Crowds came, and it seemed as though the family would soon be rich, but the authorities stepped in and forbade the exhibitions. Since the baby needed constant attention, which the parents were unable to give, she died at the age of eight months.

Double-bodied people are perhaps the most remarkable of all freaks. They represent legal, religious (do they have two souls or one?) and psychological problems, as well as being incredibly grotesque. They are twins—or sometimes triplets—who did not divide. The best known are the so-called Siamese twins, twins connected by a bond of flesh. Often the twins are not two distinct people. Like little Rita-Christina, they may be divided at the waist or may have two heads or two faces or four legs or have a body growing out of one twin's chest or any other combination. Sometimes united twins can be separated by an operation, but more often it is impossible without killing one or both.

United twins almost always differ strongly in personality—far more than do ordinary twins. Dr Robert Harris, who studied a number of such cases, came to the conclusion that "united twins, as a rule, . . . are unlike in physical conformation, in measures of health and strength and in mental characteristics." There is only one characteristic that they share: they are invariably of the same sex.

As is to be expected when two people are chained together for life and in addition frequently have conflicting temperaments, united twins often quarrel. This causes weird and rather pitiful situations. A famous pair of united twins was the Scottish brothers who lived in the court of James III in the late 1400s. The brothers were divided at the waist with two bodies and one pair of legs. This type of divided twins is called dicephalus. The twins were born near Glasgow and were brought to the court at an early age, living there for twenty-eight years. They used to sing duets, one singing tenor and the other bass. They did not get along well together and often had fights, one set of arms against the other. There is no record of who won.

An even more grotesque and tragic case was Edward Mordake, a remarkably handsome young man who was gifted as a musician and a scholar. In addition, he was heir to a peerage. One would think that Edward had everything going for him and so he did—with one exception. On the back of his head he had another face. It was said to be that of a girl, although in cases of united twins both are always of the same sex. The head was functional, though it could not eat or speak. The eyes moved and followed the motions of anyone in the room. The face could also laugh and cry. Edward became obsessed with his "devil twin," as he called it. He demanded that it be removed even if the operation killed him, but no doctor would undertake the delicate surgery involved. At last, Edward shut himself up in a suite of rooms, refusing to see anyone, even his own family. He claimed that at night the face would whisper awful things to him in his sleep, "such things as they only speak of in hell." Unable to stand the strain, he killed himself at age twenty-three.

Curiously, in 1917, there was a Mexican named Pasqual Piñon, born with an extra head growing out of his forehead. As with Mordake, the head could move its eyes and obviously could see, and the mouth could open and shut, although it was not able to speak. I have been told that eventually the head became inoperative and was simply a lifeless excrescence.

In spite of the terrible strain under which they must live, united twins do not always dislike each other. In some cases, the bond between them is even stronger than the bond of flesh. Such a couple was Margaret and Mary Gibb, American Siamese twins joined just above the buttocks. Their personalities were very different. Mary was overweight, easy-going and carefree; Margaret was thin, high-strung and continually worrying. Despite these differences, the girls were devoted to each other. To separate the girls would have been comparatively easy. Neither felt the other's pain, and their circulatory systems were largely separate. However, the girls firmly refused to be separated. "This is the way we were born and this is the way we want to live," they protested. They appeared in vaudeville doing a song-and-dance act and made enough to open a gift shop in their hometown of Holyoke, Massachusetts. After it closed in 1949, they retired and lived in near-seclusion.

In 1966, it was found that Margaret had cancer that was spreading rapidly. Now it seemed certain that the girls must be cut apart, because a few small arterial branches in their common bond were bringing Margaret's infected blood into Mary's body. Yet the girls still refused. "We have lived together, so let us die together," they insisted. In June, 1967, they died within two minutes of each other. They were fifty-four years old.

United twins have enabled medical

science to solve several important problems. There is a vast amount of information on Chang and Eng, the original Siamese twins, in the files of the College of Physicians and Surgeons in Philadelphia. Irina-Galina, a double-headed baby who lived a hundred years ago in Europe, provided the solution to the old controversy as to whether we sleep because our bodies or our brains are tired. As the baby's heads slept at different times, it was shown that the brain is the important factor.

United twins have also raised some curious legal problems. The famous Bo-hemian Twins, Rosa and Josepha Blazek, born in Skerychova, Bohemia, in 1878, created a legal controversy that lasted for years. The girls were Siamese twins; both had the same anus, although they had separate vaginas. Everyone remarked on how different the girls were in their behavior and mannerisms. Rosa was quick-witted and a good talker, while Josepha was slower and quieter. One would often be awake while her twin slept. One liked beer and the other preferred wine. Rosa liked salads, which her sister detested. They were hungry and thirsty at different

Rosa and Josepha Balzek, Siamese twins. The child is Rosa's. The father offered to marry her but the courts refused, saying it would be bigamy. Josefa was always very shocked at her sister's act, although Rosa claimed she enjoyed the seduction as much as she did. They could experience mutual sensations through the connecting bond.

Rosa and Josepha Balzek shown nude.

times, but if one was given a drug, both reacted. Rosa was by far the stronger and often pulled her reluctant sister around.

In 1910, Rosa gave birth to a baby boy. The father wanted to marry her, but the courts forbade it on the grounds that it would be bigamy. Josepha was indignant at her sister's conduct. Rosa claimed this was gross hypocrisy on her part, since she had enjoyed the seduction as much as Rosa. The sisters were still alive in 1921, traveling with circuses. Rosa's child went with them.

Josepha's claim that she was ignorant of Rosa's behavior is not quite as incredible as it sounds. All united twins develop the ability to divorce themselves mentally from the other so as to create the illusion of privacy. Several twins have discussed this power and claim that they can completely block out the other's presence. If they didn't, they would probably go mad.

Another curious legal tangle occurred a few years ago in Germany. A businessman had one of a pair of Siamese twins arrested in a legal dispute, only to have the other twin sue him for false arrest. It is problems of this kind that Mark Twain makes capital of in his novel, *Those Extraordinary Twins* (which later became *Pudd'nhead Wilson*). Twain was actually thinking of the Tocci twins, whom we'll discuss later.

Another pair of Siamese twins who said they could completely separate themselves mentally was Daisy and Violet Hilton. They were born in England in 1908 and were joined at the buttocks. As their mother rejected them, they were "adopted" by a Mrs Mary Hilton, whom they were taught to call "aunt," and took her name. Mrs Hilton made a fortune exhibiting the children, first in Europe and then in the United States. When Mrs Hilton died, her daughter and her husband took over the remunerative business of exhibiting the children.

According to statements the girls made later, this couple ruthlessly exploited them until finally they learned of their legal rights and brought suit for their freedom. Percilla Bejano, the "monkey-girl," used to play with the sisters when they were all ten or twelve years old and working in a carnival together. "They were never ill-treated," Percilla assured me. "They were given the best of educations and lived very comfortably. Years later, they got into the hands of a shrewd lawyer who dreamed up the suit." Be that as it may, the court agreed with the sisters. Their contract was canceled and their guardians were forced to pay them a sum so large that the girls could have been financially independent for life. This was in 1931.

The girls were probably the highest-paid freaks on record; their weekly earnings may have reached five thousand dollars. They went to Hollywood and made two motion pictures: *Freaks*, and later the story of their lives released under the title of *Chained for Life*. But the girls seemed to have had no idea how to handle money. They had a succession of lovers who cheated them far more than their guardians had done. One girl dyed her hair blonde so her boyfriend could tell her from her sister. Both girls married and both divorced. They hated carnival life. Joseph Hilton, the old-time showman (no relation to the girls), knew them well. He told me they were pleasant but rather stiff, "being English" as he expressed it. Of course, their sex life fascinated people and the girls explained that they could, at will, shut off all knowledge of the other's actions so that one girl could be having sexual relations with a lover without her sister's knowing it.

I talked to Anton LaVey, who spent many years in side shows and circuses and knew the girls well. He doubted this statement. "I had the strong impression that the girls shared mutual sensations. If one smelt a certain odor, so did the other. I think they were jealous of each other's husband; if one girl was having sexual relations, her sister might be enjoying it more than she did. They were rivals in everything and completely dependent on each other. With the knowledge of surgery that then existed, I do not believe they could have been cut apart. But besides the physical problem there was an even stronger psychological difficulty. The sisters had grown so used to sharing sensations that if they had been separated, they would have been lost. You know that if a man has his leg amputated, he may still be convinced that he feels pain in his toes. If the sisters had been divided, I doubt if they could ever have grown reconciled to losing the other's responses. It would have been like losing part of your brain."

Unhappily, the sisters sank lower and lower both financially and as performers. At one time, they were giving demonstrations of skin lotions in front of drug stores. In 1969, they were working in a drive-in grocery in Charlotte, North Carolina. They had been stranded in Charlotte five years before while on a promotional tour for their picture, *Chained for Life*. On January 6, they failed to report for work. The store owner notified the police, who broke down the door of their modest home and found the famous sisters dead of complications resulting from influenza. They had made and lost several fortunes. Perhaps their numerous love affairs were a desperate desire to prove that in spite of their condition they could attract men.

Probably the rarest of all united twins are the dicephalus; like the Scottish twins they are divided at the waist with one pair of legs but two separate trunks. Such a pair was the Tocci twins, born in Locarno, Italy, in 1877. They had the same abdomen,

same anus and same penis, two trunks, two heads and four arms. Their delighted parents promptly exhibited them at Turin, and shortly were making the equivalent of one thousand dollars a week from the babies, which to simple peasants seemed like a fortune. The twins toured Europe, causing a sensation wherever they appeared. The one on the right was named Giovanni Batista and the one on the left Giacomo.

As is usually the case, the twins had entirely different personalities. Giovanni was the more intelligent and a good artist. Giacomo was rather dull and possessed no artistic talent. Since each mind controlled one leg, they were unable to walk, although they could stand. They were forced to hold their central arms straight up, because there was not room enough between their bodies for the arms to bend naturally. They were brought to the United States when in their teens and drew such crowds that soon they had enough money to retire. As neither boy enjoyed show business, they bought a secluded villa in Italy and disappeared from public life.

After seeing a poster of the Tocci twins, Mark Twain was inspired to write the novel, *Those Extraordinary Twins*. Obviously, Twain knew of the trouble that the twins had walking and of their quite different natures. In his book, Twain solves the first problem by supposing that each twin has control over both legs for a week. One boy is a teetotaler and the other a heavy drinker, but as the drinker has a good head for liquor, it is the abstentious twin who gets drunk. He also describes one as a coward while the other rushed into danger. The aggressive twin kicks a man and the question before the court is to prove which twin did the kicking. Except for the miraculous change of control over the legs, all these problems could well have happened to united twins.

There is a pair of dicephalus twin girls living today in Russia, where they are wards of the state. Their names are Masha and Dasha, born January 4, 1950, and they are quite pretty girls. They are under the care of physiologist Pyotr Anokhin, who studies the girls both from a medical and psychiatric point of view. Like the Tocci twins, each girl controls one leg. For a long time they could not walk, but by the time they were five, under Dr Anokhin's tutelage, they learned to coordinate their movements, so they can now not only walk but ride a bicycle, dance and even climb a ladder.

The twins are quite different mentally. Dasha is smarter and more aggressive than her sister, although they have identical genes and have naturally always shared the same environment. Their circulatory system is interconnected, but though their spines are connected at the coccyx, their spinal cords are separate. As a result, their senses of touch are totally distinct. They become ill separately and fall asleep

Lentini with his manager.

Frank Lentini, the three-legged man from Italy, with his father. He has lived in America since the age of ten.

separately. They have only one bladder, so sometimes one twin wants to urinate and the other doesn't. They have a common reproductive system and could become a mother.

With some united twins, there is only one person, but he—or she—has extra organs belonging to the undeveloped twin. Such a twin was Frank Lentini, who is well remembered by many people in show business. Lentini was the result of non-separating triplets. He had three legs, two sets of genital organs, four feet and sixteen toes. His third leg grew out of the base of his spine. Lentini was a great fisherman, and he used his third leg as a stool to sit on while waiting for a bite. His legs were all different. One leg was thirty-nine inches long, one thirty-eight inches and one thirty-six inches. So, as he used to complain, "Even though I have three legs, I don't have a pair."

Frank was born in Sicily in 1889. When the midwife saw the baby, she was so horrified that she threw it under the bed and ran out of the room. His parents simply refused to admit that the baby existed and Frank was raised by an aunt. He had eleven brothers and sisters, all normal. As a child, he was desperately unhappy until one day his aunt took him to an institution for hopelessly crippled children and Frank decided that he was comparatively well off. As he later explained, "I could walk, see, use my hands, talk and do many things those poor children could not." At an early age, he went into show business and came to America in 1898. For years he was

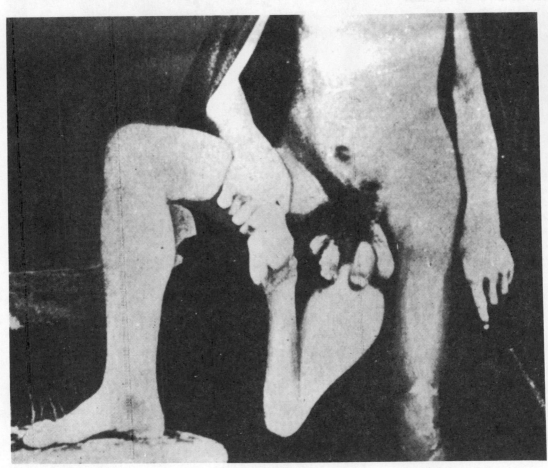

Frank Lentini has three legs and double sexual organs. One of his acts consisted of kicking a football across the stage with his third leg.

Myrtle Corbin, the four-legged woman from Clebourne, Texas. She was double-bodied from the waist down and had twenty toes and four legs. On the right she is shown with her husband and a daughter. She had four girls and a boy. According to her promoter three were born from one body and two from the other. The photo above was taken in 1907.

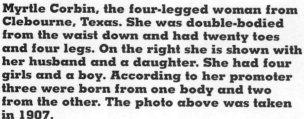

the acknowledged king of freaks. Only Myrtle Corbin, the four-legged woman, was considered more remarkable. During his act, Lentini kicked a football the length of the sideshow tent with his third leg.

Joseph Hilton told me, "Frank was one of the best-natured men I ever knew. He would take half an hour to answer a child's question if he thought the youngster was sincerely interested. He loved kids and had four of his own: three boys and a girl. He was a great cook and his wife raised herbs in pots which she kept in the window of their trailer because he refused to use dried herbs. He was a fine swimmer and used his third leg as a rudder."

Lentini became so successful that he ran his own ten-in-one side-show. Like most

Laloo in 1897 when he was 18 years old. Originally from India, he had a parasitic twin attached to his body. He was killed in a train wreck while traveling in Mexico with the Norris and Rowe Circus in 1905.

Another Indian Siamese twin, Perumal Sami, was born in 1888. This photo was taken in 1915 on his final tour of the US before he returned to his native land. He had his own Indian cooks and would not eat anything unless they personally cooked it for him—he did not trust American food.

great stars, Lentini was proud of his fame and susceptible to flattery. Ward Hall remembers, "Once I was on tour with Pete Terhune [the versatile dwarf performer] and we joined a carny where Frank was playing with his ten-in-one. I had a bannerline with dwarfs dancing on broken glass, doing fire-eating, climbing a ladder of sharp swords in bare feet and so on. Everyone thought I had a whole troupe of dwarfs and I didn't deny it, but actually Pete was doing all the acts. After we opened, the owner of the carny came around and said Frank was complaining that my show conflicted with his. 'He says you've got a five-in-one so you'll have to close,' the owner informed me. I said, 'I

know Frank pretty well. Let me talk to him.' I went to Frank and for once he was really angry and started bawling me out. When he'd finished, I said, 'But, Frank, no one comes to your show to see fire-eating, sword-swallowing or any of the other acts. They only come to see the great Frank Lentini.' Frank stopped shouting at me, thought it over and then said, 'Ward, of course you're right. There's no conflict. Now why didn't I realize that?' There was no more trouble after that."

Myrtle Corbin was the only freak who could challenge Lentini as a box office attraction. She had the body of a twin growing between her legs. The body was well-developed from the waist down and completely functional. She was billed as "the woman from Texas with four legs." Myrtle was married and, according to her billing, had five children—three from her own body and two from the twin's. This is unlikely but not impossible. The *British Medical Journal* of 1889 describes a young woman of twenty who had a similar twin growing just above her waist. She was married, and when her family physician informed her that she was pregnant, replied, "I think you are mistaken. If it had been on my right side [the twin], I would have believed it." The doctor found that her husband usually had intercourse with the twin. The twin could not deliver the baby and it had to be aborted.

Perhaps the best-known individual who had a parasitic twin was Laloo, a Hindu, born in Oovonin, Oudh, in 1874. He traveled widely in Europe and America and has been written up in many medical textbooks. Laloo's twin was headless, attached to his body by the neck. It had two arms and two legs and Laloo could tell wherever it was touched. The twin was, of course, a male and could pass urine and get an erection, but for publicity purposes it was advertised as a girl in order to add even more to the interest.

The most tragic case of a parasitic twin was Betty Lou Williams, a black girl and the child of poor sharecroppers, who had a twin sister growing out of her side. When she was very young, Betty Lou was taken over by the famous showman, Dick Best, who made a fortune for her and from her. I have talked to a number of people who knew Betty Lou and they all agree she was one of the most generous and best-natured

Betty Lou Williams was born in 1932 in Albany, Georgia. This photo was taken at the Chicago World's Fair, "Believe It Or Not Show," 1934. She has a parasitic appendage growing out of her side. X-rays show the head of another child embedded inside Betty's body.

of people. Percilla describes her as "always laughing." She built her parents a forty-thousand-dollar house and bought a farm for them. She also sent her brothers and sisters through college. Betty Lou could well afford to do it since she was paid

$250 a week; in addition, money from the sale of her pictures came to around $500—a large sum in the thirties.

When she was twenty-one, Betty Lou fell deeply in love with a man who, although he had no hesitation in accepting money from her, refused to marry her and finally deserted her. Betty Lou died of a broken heart. I realize this sounds melodramatic, but three people who knew her intimately assured me that it was so. Betty Lou was pretty, intelligent and charming—except for her deformity. It made her rich, but it also killed her.

Undoubtedly, the most famous united twins of all time—who gave the popular name to all united twins—were Chang and Eng, the original Siamese twins, born in the little village of Meklong, Siam, in 1811. They were attached at the chest by a narrow band of cartilage about 5 inches long. At first, the boys could only stand facing each other, but with long practice and encouragement by their mother, they were able to stretch the connecting band until they could stand side by side. A British merchant named Robert Hunter, one of the few Europeans allowed in Siam at that time, saw the boys swimming in the river and thought at first they were some sort of strange sea animal. Later, he spoke to them and was greatly impressed by the twins' pleasant manners and quick wits. A shrewd businessman, Hunter conceived of the idea of taking the twins abroad and exhibiting them. His request was refused both by the boys' mother and the king, who felt that exporting such an oddity would give the country a bad name; in fact, when the boys were born, a former king had seriously considered having them killed as evil monsters. Hunter, however, was able to form a partnership with an American sea captain named Abel Coffin, and the two men offered the mother such a large

sum that she was unable to refuse, especially since she was a widow with many other children. Hunter persuaded the king that the twins would make Siam world-famous, which indeed they did; the Siamese have a rather bitter proverb that states their country is known for nothing but cats, white elephants and twins.

These Korean twins are joined at the breastbone, 1903.

The twins had very different temperaments, as seems usual in such cases. Chang was more aggressive and quick-tempered. Eng was quiet and allowed his brother to dominate him. As children, they once had such a violent fight that their mother was afraid they would injure each other. Gradually, they developed great self-control. Although not more than five feet three inches tall, they were remarkably strong. They were also rapid learners, picking up English easily and becoming so skillful at checkers, and later chess, that few opponents could beat them. They were able to somersault and turn back-flips as well as perform other tumbling feats that seemed incredible.

In America, enormous crowds turned out to see them even at the then-extravagant admission price of six dollars. After a fabulously successful tour, they went to England, where their success was repeated. Hunter and Coffin wanted to show them in France, but the French government refused, fearful that if a pregnant woman saw them she might give birth to united twins. Still, other countries did not share this superstition and the twins did well. Hunter dropped out of the partnership and Coffin bought out his share of the profits. From all accounts, Coffin swindled the boys out of their share of the profits. At least, the twins thought so, and when they were twenty-one and of age, they tore up the contract making them Coffin's wards and set out on their own.

The boys turned out to be excellent businessmen and acquired a small fortune. In Alabama, a doctor in the audience stood up and demanded that he be allowed to examine them. The twins told him he could do so in the privacy of their dressing room but not in public, whereupon the doctor leaped on the stage and, turning to the audience, accused them of being fakes.

Chang promptly kicked him. The doctor sued Chang for assault. At the trial, the twins' lawyer pointed out that there was no way the doctor could prove whether he had been kicked by Chang or Eng. The judge admitted this difficulty, but insisted that no matter who had done the kicking, the doctor had certainly been kicked and insisted that the twins post a bond to keep the peace. Undoubtedly, this incident gave Mark Twain the idea for the fictional lawsuit described in *Those Extraordinary Twins*.

The boys were noted for their quick wit, and part of their act was to exchange jokes with the audience as some stand-up comedians do today. Far from feeling sensitive about their condition, they made fun of it. Once they got on a train wrapped in a cloak, and when the conductor came to collect the tickets, Chang handed him a ticket but Eng refused to pay. "Then I'll have to put you off the train," threatened the conductor. "Go ahead, but if you put me off and I have a ticket, I'll sue the company," retorted Chang. They then threw back the cloak, revealing themselves as the famous twins, to the great delight of the passengers.

The boys exhibited themselves in Barnum's famous museum, although they did not get along well with the master showman, whom they suspected of shortchanging them. Even so, they made a large sum of money both for themselves and for Barnum. In 1837, being in their middle twenties and independently wealthy, they bought a farm in Wilkesboro, North Carolina. Naturally, they soon became local celebrities, not only because of their physical conformation but because of their astonishing strength and ingenuity. They built their own house, cutting down trees to do it, and are credited with inventing the "double-stroke" with an axe—one twin always striking at a forty-five-degree angle to his right and the other doing the same to his left. Since then this double-stroke technique has been adopted by teams of wood choppers, saving them the need to change their grip. The twins were so strong that they were able to lift the whole house at one corner and settle it on the foundation. The house still stands.

The twins fell in love with two sisters, Sarah and Adelaide Yates, the daughters of a neighboring farmer. The farmer had no objections and, clearly, the girls were deeply in love with the curious brothers. Others in the rural community felt differently. Such a union struck many of the mountaineers as both unnatural and immoral. The twins were threatened with mob action if the double marriage went through. Desperate, the twins went to the College of Physicians and Surgeons in Philadelphia and begged that they be separated, even if it meant their death. There were no X-rays in those days and the surgeons could only apply what tests they knew. It was impossible to tell what organs were in the connecting bond. If it were touched near Chang, only he could feel it, if near Eng, only he responded. But if the cord were touched in the middle, both twins were conscious of it. Even if the twins were sleeping and the bond was touched in the center—where, curiously, the twins had a mutual navel—they both awoke. At first, the surgeons refused to operate, but when the twins insisted they reluctantly agreed.

All arrangements had been made when the two girls suddenly appeared. They had heard what was planned and tearfully begged the brothers not to endanger their lives. After a pathetic scene, all four were married in a double ceremony and returned to Wilkesboro. Faced with a *fait accompli*, the community accepted the situation.

The strange marriages were highly successful. The twins fathered twenty-two children. They built separate houses for their families and agreed to spend three days in each. Each twin was to be the complete master in his own home and the other had to agree to everything he wished to do. They adhered to this agreement so strictly that eventually it was to be the indirect cause of their death.

Some such arrangement was necessary because the twins frequently disagreed. Once while on a hay wagon, they had such a violent argument that Chang shouted furiously, "If you don't keep quiet, I'll throw you off this wagon!" An instant later, he realized the absurdity of his statement and both brothers burst out laughing.

Although the twins might quarrel with each other, they stood together against any outsider. They hired a man to help them shingle a roof and, when the man failed to appear, went ahead with the shingling themselves. A few hours later, the man drove up, dead drunk, and shouted, "Get off that roof, you yoke of oxen, and let a human being do the job." The twins got off the roof—fast—and proceeded to give the drunk a beating that sobered him up.

The Civil War ruined the brothers as it did virtually all Southerners with property. They were forced to go back into show business, but now they were elderly men who could not do the somersaults and back-flips that had so delighted the crowds. Even so, they were able to make a comfortable sum of money before returning to Wilkesboro. Chang had always been more intemperate in his habits than the quiet Eng and now he began to drink heavily; so heavily, in fact, that Eng was alarmed. He had cause to be, for Chang suffered a stroke that left him partly paralyzed. Now it was Eng who became the stronger, more dominant member of the team, but even so he could not stop his brother's drinking—at least not when they were staying in Chang's home.

In January, 1874, Chang developed a serious case of bronchitis while at his home. When the three days were over, Eng suggested that for once they break their rule and not travel over the roads to his home in an open buggy. Chang, who had been drinking immoderately, insisted on their rigid custom, so the brothers started off. When they arrived at Eng's home, Chang had taken a bad chill which developed into what was later found to be pneumonia. That night as they lay in bed together, Eng suddenly woke. At first, he did not know what the trouble was. Then he realized that his brother had stopped breathing. Unable to move, he could only lie there shouting for help until one of his sons heard him and came in. "Something is wrong with your uncle," Eng told him. The boy examined the still figure and said gravely, "Uncle Chang is dead." "Then I am going too," said his father and burst into tears.

A surgeon was hurriedly sent for in the desperate hope that he could cut apart the twins. But he arrived too late. Eng died shortly after his brother. They were sixty-three years old.

The bodies were taken to the Mutter Museum in the College of Physicians and Surgeons in Philadelphia and an autopsy performed. It was found that Chang had died of a cerebral clot and Eng, to the doctors' amazement, apparently had died of fright. The shock of his brother's death had been too much for him. The autopsy showed that the twins shared a joint circulatory system and with the medical knowledge then available probably could not have been separated.

The house Chang and Eng built at Wilkesboro still stands. The twins are buried in nearby White Plains. They left many descendants, including a president of the Union Pacific Railroad and a major general in the Air Force. Many of the twins' grandchildren and great-grandchildren continue to farm in the Wilkesboro area.

With modern surgery, it is possible to separate Siamese twins today under conditions that would have seemed impossible even twenty years ago; in fact, to a layman they seem impossible now. In September, 1974, an operation was performed on Siamese twins from the Dominican Republic that attracted worldwide attention. The twins were girls, the daughters of Mr and Mrs Salvador Rodriguez, who came to America in hopes of having the children cut apart. The sixteen-month-old babies were joined at the pelvis and shared genital organs. Incredible as it seems, they had four vaginas and only one anus between them. They also had one colon. The operation was performed at Children's Hospital of Philadelphia. A team of twenty-three surgeons, headed by Dr C. Everett Koop, took ten and one half hours to separate the children. Meanwhile, the lobby of the hospital was packed with TV crews and reporters, not only from America but also Europe. At 3 pm Dr Koop came out of the operating room and told the crowd, "Everything is all right. All things being equal, the kids will grow up to get married and have children." The papers called it the "miracle on 34th Street."

The twins were named Clara and Alta. As they had only one colon, part of Alta's bowel had to be used to make a colon for Clara. Later, additional surgery was needed on the pelvic bones so the children could walk.

To the inhabitants of the little village of San Jose de Ochoa where they were born, the twins were heroines. When news came that the operation had been successful and the twins were coming home, a great fiesta was prepared. All the houses were specially painted for the occasion. Five thousand people arrived, riding everything from ancient Land Rovers to donkeys, and a feast was prepared with turkey, pork and chicken. Alas, at the last moment Alta, always the weaker of the two, came down with a virus and the celebration had to be postponed. However, Alta made a speedy recovery and now both girls are at home with their parents.

The pride and excitement in the community showed that freaks are not always considered a disgrace, but can be regarded as valuable assets capable of attracting international notice.

Perhaps of all freaks, united twins have the hardest problems to face, for they must suffer together and not alone. They can never have an instant of real privacy and are always bound to one another's often incompatible natures. Yet many have led happy and useful lives, and have contributed to medical knowledge.

Two poses of Siamese twins born in Maine, 1940. They only lived a few hours.

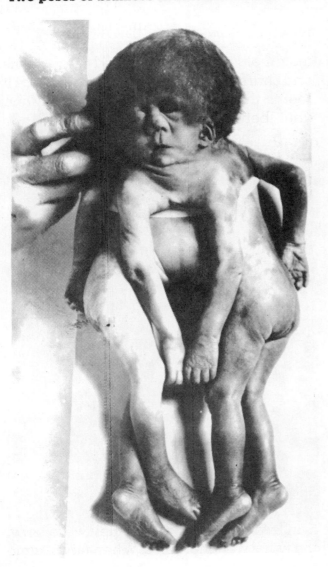 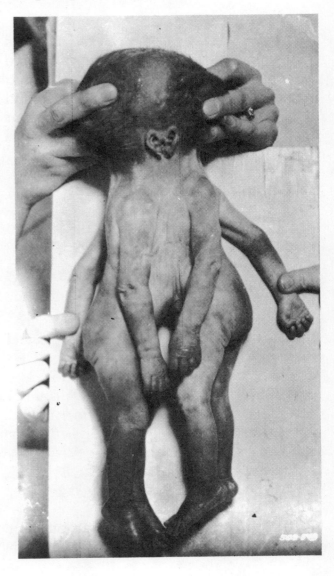

6

Mother, Am I a Boy or a Girl?

Ward Hall told me, "No doubt about it, the greatest attraction for the blow-off was a half-and-half [a hermaphrodite]. I remember one I had—Diana De Elgar. I ran a marquee from the blow-off to the bally platform [the platform outside a real side show where the talker introduces some of the performers to the crowd to induce them to go inside]. After the talker gave his pitch, a spotlight would hit Diana and she would walk slowly from the blow-off under the marquee to the bally. Diana was dressed in a Dior gown and carried a fan. She would explain that she was half man and

Aileen, a hermaphrodite, born in 1907.

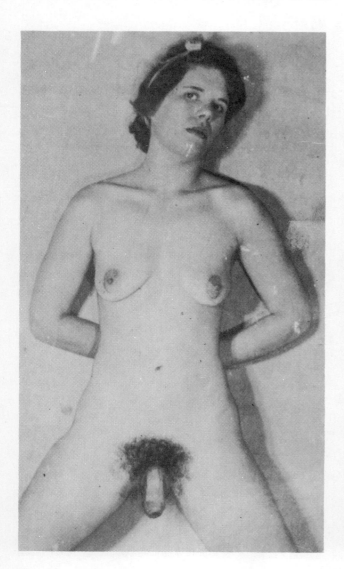

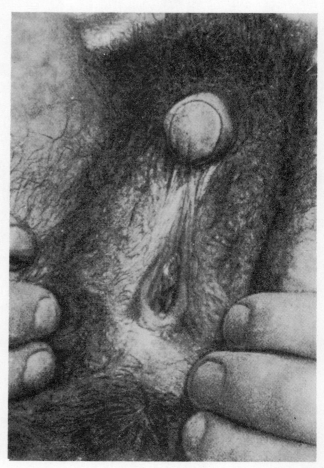

half woman. 'How can this be?' you will ask. 'In the tent, I will show myself completely naked and you can see for yourselves.' Then the talker would explain that the show would allow any doctor in the audience to examine Diana, and was prepared to pay one hundred dollars if she was not as advertised. Then he'd turn the tip [bring the crowd into the tent]. Damned if one night there wasn't a doctor who asked to examine Diana. I thought we were dead, as Diana was a grift [a fake]. But after the doctor examined him, he said that Diana was a genuine hermaphrodite, the first he'd ever seen. That shows you how skillful Diana was—that he could fool a doctor."

Joseph Hilton agreed with Hall. "If you had a good half-and-half, you could run a hadgy-badgy [any kind of acts thrown together at random]. The half-and-half carried the whole show."

The word hermaphrodite comes from the Greek legend of Hermaphroditus, the son of Hermes and Aphrodite, who joined with a wood nymph who loved him and became both man and woman. Although most half-and-halfs were grifts, some did have the external features of both a man and a woman. I have been assured by a doctor who has studied such cases that technically there is no such thing as a person who possesses both functional sexes; that is, one who can give birth to a child as a woman and also father children as a man. However, there are a very few cases of an individual who possesses neither testicles nor ovaries but "ovatestes," which are a combination of both. Such people are sterile, but they are "true" hermaphrodites. Most so-called hermaphrodites are really either men or women, but are so developed that they seem to have the organs of the other sex. Some can even deceive doctors.

The Jon-Mae Arcy pair were both double-sexed and toured the country about 1915. Jon (rear) was double-sexed horizontally, below the waist was male and above, female. Mae (front) was double-sexed vertically. Notice the difference in breast and muscular development.

I think I had better define some terms now, if not in proper medical language at least in a way that the layman can understand.

Homosexual. A person who is sexually attracted to members of the same sex.

Transvestite. A person who has a compulsive desire to impersonate members of the opposite sex. A transvestite is not necessarily homosexual. He (they are usually men) never regards himself as a woman and does not wish to become one, although he dresses as a woman and imitates feminine mannerisms.

Transsexual. A transsexual usually regards himself "as a woman trapped in the body of a man" (very few women are transsexuals). The transsexual does want to become a woman and will often submit to painful and expensive surgery to turn himself into a woman, which he regards as his rightful role. The transsexual is not always homosexual. Even when as a result of surgery he has become a woman, he may have no sexual interest in men.

The most famous transvestite in history was the remarkable Chevalier d'Eon, who had a profound effect on European politics in the eighteenth century. The chevalier was born in Burgundy to the wife of a prominent lawyer. Baptized Genevieve,

Josephine, born in Austria, shown here at age 19.

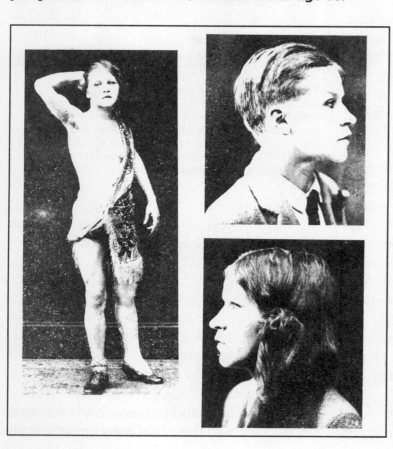

the child was raised as a girl to the age of three. Then the parents, apparently deciding that they had made a mistake, dressed their offspring as a boy and later sent him to a military school. Seemingly, young d'Eon was a case of pseudo-hermaphroditism, the name given to the physical state in which the male organs do not appear until late. However, the chevalier never had to shave and resembled a pretty young girl rather than a boy. The resemblance was so marked that the French courtiers, as a joke, introduced d'Eon to Louis XV, who attempted the expected royal seduction to his subsequent embarrassment. But the king saw a use for the strange youth and sent him to Russia as a secret agent, where he quickly gained the favor of the Empress Elizabeth, a lady of versatile interests in sexual matters. D'Eon acted as a highly efficient spy for Louis who, in appreciation, made him a captain of dragoons. Despite his girlish appearance, the chevalier proceeded to distinguish himself in combat and acquired the reputation of being the deadliest duelist in Europe.

France had been disastrously defeated by England in a series of long, bloody wars and had to sue for peace. Louis sent the young dragoon captain to England as his special agent to arrange the terms and d'Eon caused a sensation. The betting on his sex ran into thousands of pounds and became so serious that at Lloyd's Coffee House (which eventually became the famous insurance house of Lloyd's of London) it was feared that if the matter were ever settled, so much money would change hands as to cause a national panic. Husbands urged their wives and fathers urged their daughters to seduce the chevalier and solve the mystery. Gamblers hired ruffians to waylay him, but d'Eon was immune to female wiles and too capable a swordsman to be attacked. He succeeded in arranging the notorious Peace of Paris on terms so favorable to France that John Wilkes said angrily, "This must indeed be the peace of God, for it passes human understanding." In 1745, the chevalier was involved in the Scottish invasion of England under Bonnie Prince Charlie. During this period of diplomacy and machination, d'Eon did so much for France that Beaumarchais, the great dramatist, described him as "a second Jeanne d'Arc" to which Voltaire, who despised the man-woman, retorted, "Yes, and he should meet the same fate."

When Louis XV died, d'Eon fell from favor. He then blackmailed Louis XVI by threatening to make public letters from Louis XV's court, proving that France had supported the Scottish uprising. Louis agreed to grant d'Eon a yearly income of twelve thousand livres with the understanding that from then on d'Eon would always dress as a woman. The chevalier agreed, although he still kept up his swordsmanship and was often seen at Angelo's famous fencing salon in hoop skirt and wig, thrusting away. He died in 1810 at the age of eighty-two, universally accepted as a woman until the doctor who had attended him lifted up the sheet covering the corpse and staggered back with the cry, "It's a man!" D'Eon's great mystery had at last been solved, but now no one cared.

In recent years, there have been several transsexuals who attracted international attention as the result of having changed themselves into women by surgery. The most widely publicized of these was George W. Jorgensen, the twenty-six-year-old ex-GI who went to Denmark in 1952 since no American doctor would perform the procedure. It took five major operations, one minor and two thousand hormone injections to turn George into Christine. A Copenhagen air force sergeant who dated Christine was quoted as saying, "She has the best body of any girl I ever saw." Even more remarkable was Robert Cowell, an English fighter pilot in World War II. Married and the father of two children, he became Roberta Cowell and claims to have become "a woman physically, psychologically and glandularly." Cowell emphasizes that he never had any homosexual tendencies.

Actually, neither of these man really became a woman, being unable to menstruate or bear children. They are simply castrated men.

In carnies, the half-and-half is always publicized as being divided laterally: the right side male and the left side female. This goes back to an old folk belief that the right side of any individual is the strong or masculine side and the left the weak or feminine side. Male babies are supposedly conceived by sperm from the right testicle. There is, of course, no basis for this superstition whatsoever. Hermaphrodites are very seldom divided laterally, although it does sometimes happen that the person has an ovary on one side and a testicle on the other. Ward Hall says he knew of only one such individual—Ester Lester. Much more commonly, the half-and-half is a man whose testicles did not descend and are still in the body (what stockmen call a "Risling" when it occurs among colts or bulls). He may also have an extremely small, gutted penis that resembles a clitoris. A woman may have an enlarged clitoris that cannot be readily told from a penis and the labia may be fused to resemble a scrotum. In such cases, the child may grow up accepted as a member of the opposite sex.

In 1824, Catherine Hoffman, who had been married twenty years, left her husband and married a woman, changing her name to Charles. It turned out that Catherine was really a man.

Adelaide Préville spent all her life as a woman and married, but never had children. After her death, the body was dissected and it was found she really was a man.

In some cases, not even the doctors can be sure. There was the famous case of Marie Dorothée which occurred in 1803. Marie stood to inherit a large estate if she was a man; if a woman, she got nothing. She was examined by five doctors. Two said she was a girl, three said a boy. A sixth was called in. He said she was both. How the case was decided, I don't know.

Sometimes with the help of surgery, the person can be swung either way. In the case of an infant, the parents decide which sex it shall belong to. If the discovery is not made until later, the individual decides for himself or herself.

There are other conditions that create a hermaphrodite or a pseudo-hermaphrodite. A child may be deficient in sex chromosomes. Normally a male has an XY chromosome and a female an XX. But one chromosome may be defective, or there may be a person with an XXY or an XYY chromosome. Another factor is hormones. Both men and women secrete both estrogen and androgen, but normal males have a much larger amount of androgen ("the male hormone") than do women. If a man happens to secrete estrogen, he develops breasts like a woman and large buttocks.*

Joseph Hall told me he once showed a half-and-half named Elsie Stick who had "breasts like a *Playboy* centerfold." Elsie was happily married to a man with the show. While the carny was playing Alabama, she died. Her husband went to claim the body only to find himself arrested. The coroner had ruled that Elsie was a man, and at that time there was a statute in Alabama making it a criminal offense for two men to live together. However, under these special circumstances, the court relented and Elsie's body was released to her husband.

I have said that there is no such thing as a hermaphrodite in whom both sexes function and I believe this to be true, but some come close to it. The *New York Medical Journal* of November 22, 1890, tells of a person twenty-eight years old who was arrested as a prostitute one evening, then discharged, and a few hours later arrested again—this time for rape. This person possessed both organs: a penis five and a half inches long and a vagina of four and a quarter inches. He also had a scrotum and ovaries. He—or she—told the doctors she menstruated every three weeks and not only got an erection but also discharged semen. He—or she—had intercourse indifferently with both men and women, enjoying both kinds of sex equally.

Some half-and-halves are extremely attractive. Dolly Regan (the "ossified girl") told me that she was good friends with Bobby Cork, a famous half-and-half. "We trouped together for years," Dolly explained. "When we first met, I was just getting into show business and he was very kind to me, explaining all the ropes. He was a man predominantly. He used to go on dates with girls and was quite a ladies' man. Bobby left a string of broken hearts behind him. I can't tell you if he was

---

* There is an excellent discussion not only of hermaphroditism but other sexual characteristics and their causes in *Sexual Signatures: On Being a Man or a Woman*, by John Money and Patricia Tucker (Little, Brown; Boston, 1975)

a real half-and-half or a grift because, although he used to exhibit himself naked in the blow-off, he never let me see him. 'I just don't like the idea,' he explained, so I never insisted. Bobby died of food poisoning, but he was one of the top attractions in the business."

Joseph Hilton had a half-and-half who was too darned attractive for her own good. "Once we were playing a still date," Hilton explained. (A still date means the carnival is not showing at a fair.) "The local chapter of the American Legion was backing us. The committeeman fell in love with our half-and-half. He wanted to leave his wife and children to marry her. This was especially embarrassing since the half-and-half was really a man—mostly. If they had gotten married, the committeeman would have been in for some surprises. He told his friends he was going to get a divorce and join the show. They complained to the carny's manager and he told me I'd have to get rid of the half-and-half, so I let him go. It was too bad, because he was really talented."

People who fool around with hermaphrodites often do get surprises. Frances Murphy, who weighed 220 pounds but still managed to pass for an attractive woman, was playing in New York during the World's Fair in 1939. While riding in the subway, Frances was molested by some sailors. She flattened one with a right to the jaw and was arrested for being a man in women's clothes. In court she had to prove to the judge that she really was a woman, or a reasonable facsimile thereof.

Most successful half-and-halfs in carnivals are grifts. Several showmen assured me that a female impersonator was far better as a half-and-half than a real hermaphrodite. "I never saw a real hermaphrodite who was a good performer," Ward Hall told me. "They know they're the real thing, so they just stand there and don't try to sell themselves." Joseph Hilton agreed with him. "After vaudeville closed, there were dozens of female impersonators out of work who joined carnivals. Plenty of them were more feminine than most women. In vaudeville, they'd learned how to hold an audience's attention, and they could fake their bodies so cleverly that even when stark naked you couldn't tell."

Bobby Cork from Trenton, N.J. in 1943.

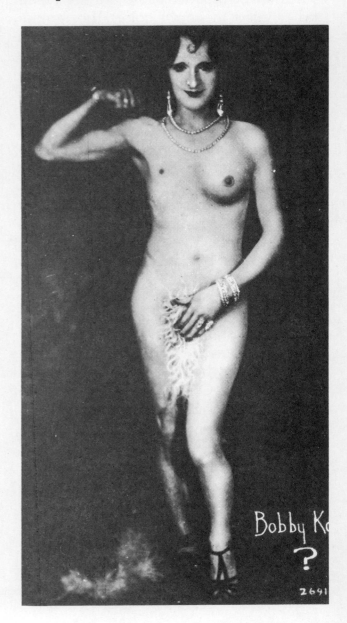

As it is traditional in carnivals for the half-and-half to be laterally divided, he must have a woman's breast on one side while the other is flat. The right arm must be muscular and the left soft and feminine. There are several ways of creating this illusion. To make a breast, a hollow rubber ball was cut in half. There is a slight indentation in the side of the ball that is hardly noticeable. When the hemisphere was turned inside out, the indentation was reversed and stood out like a nipple. It could then be glued in place with New Skin and painted the right color. The genital organs were pulled back under the crotch and held there with flesh-colored adhesive tape. A good half-and-half would exercise his right arm to make it strong, while taking care to do nothing with his left.

I once worked with a half-and-half named Francis-Francine whom I am sure was a woman. She had a penis—or an abnormally large clitoris—and had no scrotum, but possessed a vagina. Having virtually no breasts, she was forced to build up her left breast with silicone for the part. She had no scrotum, but a vagina. She was very casual about her condition, and not only posed naked but would allow members of the tip to come up and examine her closely.

Francis-Francine had been put into carnival life by her mother, who traveled with the show. One day her mother told me how she'd come to make the decision to exhibit her.

"When Francis was a baby, we seen that she was different from other kids. We didn't say nothing about it, because it's nasty to talk about such things. But the other little girls at school found out about it and they told everybody. Then the drugstore loafers used to bother her. She used to cry and cry and I'd tell her, 'Now it ain't no use cryin' so you might as well shet up.'

"When she got to be twelve years old, she had so much trouble we had to call in a doctor. I told her my other girls never had no trouble, but finally we figured it was worth five dollars to stop her screamin' with pain all the time, because my nerves ain't very strong. The doctor took her and me East to a couple of big medical exhibitions, payin' all expenses. While the doctor was showing off Francis in the clinics, I had a good time, so naturally I didn't want to go back to my husband when the show was over. I felt like it was my duty to exhibit her in sideshows on account of she's a real freak and no grift."

With the carnival, Francis-Francine must have made over five hundred a week from her cut on the blow-off, and that was big money during the Depression. She was supporting not only her mother but also a bunch of relatives who followed the show around in rickety old jalopies. She was very fond of children, but her condition prevented her from marrying—or at least she thought it did. Her relatives complained bitterly that she was swindling them by sending most of her money to children's homes.

Francis liked to give the kids who hung around the lots little presents of toys and candy. Even in women's clothes, Francis looked queer and made children nervous, so instead of handing out the gifts herself she'd have her relatives do it. Francis would stand in the background, watching with her serious, boyish face to make sure her relations didn't pouch the stuff and sell it later.

As far as I know, there are no half-and-halves showing today. The same act came to be considered too raw and got the shows in trouble with the police. Of course, there are plenty of female impersonators in show business who appear in bars and cabarets. That seems to be quite all right.

7

The Not-so-Jolly Fat People

Fat people are the bread and butter of the side show. They are seldom regarded as really great freaks, but everybody expects to see one. The crowd loves them since, in our culture at least, to be fat is to be funny. Perhaps this is because we are a nation of weight-watchers and we like to see someone worse off than we are. America holds records for fat people. In the *Guinness Book of World Records*, all three outstanding fat people are Americans.

What makes a person fat? Virtually all doctors say it is simply a case of overeating, while all fat people claim it's their glands. This can be true in certain cases. It is possible for a decreased activity of the thyroid gland to be responsible for a marked weight gain. Malfunctioning of the pituitary or adrenal gland or the ovaries can also cause a tremendous increase in weight. There is no question that some people have a tendency to gain weight easily while others remain thin, no matter how much they eat. Being inclined to put on weight myself, I especially resent my brother-in-law who, while I am toying with a spoonful of cottage cheese and a leaf of lettuce, puts away enough food to satiate a pack of ravenous hyenas and remains as thin as a yard of pump water. It's the injustice of the whole thing that infuriates me.

Do fat people eat more than others?

Here, as with giants, there seems to be no hard and fast rule. Some eat enormous

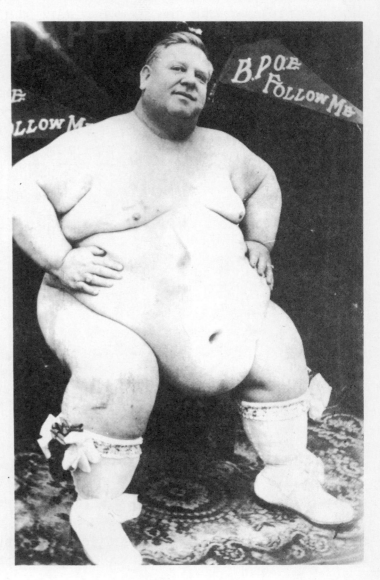

Born in Indiana, Happy Jack Eckert died in 1939. He weighed 739 pounds and had the largest belly in the world, 87 inches, but only wore a size 9 shoe.

quantities of food, while others eat somewhat less than ordinary people. One fat man (unfortunately we don't know his weight) was the Great Eater of Kent, who lived in the middle of the seventeenth century. He has been immortalized in the pamphlet, "The admirable teeth and stomach exploits of Nickolas Wood." According to this account, Mr Wood could eat a whole sheep (except, as the pamphlet fairly points out, for the skin, wool and horns). He was capable of devouring thirty pigeons at a sitting. He was said to eat as much as twenty ordinary men. After one of his meals, his belly had a tendency to split and had to be rubbed with grease to make it stretch and hold. The landlady of the White

Lion Inn swore that she saw him eat a washing bowl full of porridge, nine loaves of bread and three jugs of beer. The author of the pamphlet adds, "He holds fasting to be a most superstitious branch of Popery and hates Lent worse than a butcher,"a nice way of getting religious justification for making a hog out of himself.

Jack Biggers of Witney, England, was another tremendous eater. For a wager, he undertook to eat, in an hour, six pounds of bacon, a dish of greens, twelve suet dumplings, a loaf of bread and a gallon of beer. He came close to winning, too. He was down to two ounces of bacon and half a dumpling when he dropped dead.

On the other hand, take Edward Bright of Maldon, Essex. The last time he was weighed, in 1750, he tipped the scales at 584 pounds. He was probably over six hundred pounds when he died at age thirty. Edward was not a big eater, although he once bet that five men could fit into his coat. It turned out that seven could.

There have even been fat dwarfs. Such a one was Jimmy Camber, jester to the grandfather of James I. He was three feet high and six feet around the waist. According to tradition, Jimmy (who could not have been very bright) added an unforgettable phrase to the English language. He was on the royal yacht with his master when the fleet began to fire salutes. "What are they shooting at?" asked Jimmy anxiously. Some joker replied, "Why, at us." "Oh, may they miss!" cried Jimmy. Then the yacht started to return the salutes. "What are we firing at?" demanded Jimmy. "Why, at them," replied the same humorist. "Oh, may we hit!" exclaimed Jimmy. All through the salutes, he kept crying,

Ella Mills.

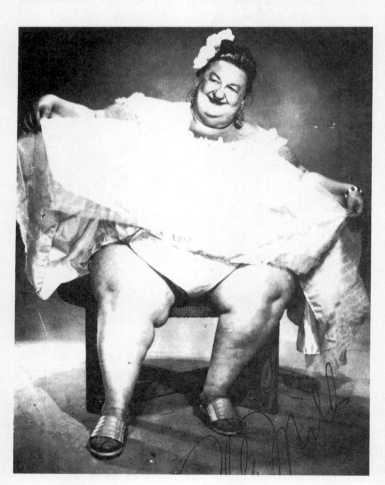

"Hit or miss, hit or miss!" and the expression caught on.

Undoubtedly in some cases—although I am convinced they are comparatively rare—abnormally fat people are simply the result of overeating. Such was unquestionably the case with Celeste Geyer, better known under her stage name of Dolly Dimples. Dolly was born in Ohio in 1901, and had no glandular problems at all; she just liked to eat. Soon she was unable to fit into her seat at school. When she graduated, she could not hold a job. The chairs were too small, the other employees ridiculed her and she couldn't get to work. It was impossible for her to fit through the turnstiles of the subway or sit in a bus. Rather curiously, she had plenty of sweethearts. Most fat women do; there are some men who like hefty girls. In 1925, Dolly married Frank Geyer. Two years later, they attended a carnival and the manager of the side show promptly hired Dolly. Her husband traveled with the show and she was launched on her career.

Dolly eventually came to weigh 550 pounds. She was making about three hundred dollars a day and with her profits built a home in Florida. It had a special concrete floor, extra-wide doors, huge chairs, a special toilet. Everything looked rosy for Dolly. Then trouble started.

She had difficulty walking, because her legs couldn't support her vast bulk. Then she had spells when she couldn't breathe. Her heart was failing her. Rushed to the hospital, the doctor told her, "Diet or die." Dolly decided to diet. By truly heroic efforts she finally got down to a trim 150 pounds. She wrote a book about her experiences and now travels around lecturing on how to lose weight. Dolly is one of the few freaks who has been able to make a successful transition from show business to private life.

In carnivals, fat people are always referred to as "jolly." Most of them seem to be, although one fat man I talked to said rather bitterly, "We have to try to laugh off our looks. We've got to be pleasant to make up for our appearance." Although most freaks are healthy, fat people are not. They have trouble walking and are prone to heart trouble, and a number have hypoglycemia. This is a condition in which the body stores too little sugar and can be serious, especially without medical help.

In addition to these problems, fat people suffer from the heat and have trouble moving. It is so difficult for them to climb up to the catwalk where they sit during the shows that they eat their meals there. Often the chair they sit on is really a commode, so they do not have to leave the catwalk all day. Women, because they wear dresses, find this simpler than do men.

Another occupational hazard for fat people is falling through floors. Several have been injured in this way. One was Baby Ruth Pontico, who was said to weigh 815 pounds. Born near Frankfort, Indiana, in 1904, she went on the stage as a young girl and married Joe Pontico, who weighed 130 pounds and sold balloons with the show. Baby Ruth always claimed that she was a light eater and her fatness was hereditary. Her mother had been a fat woman with the Ringling Brothers and weighed six hundred pounds, while her father was 255 pounds. She was famous for her generosity and was the "softest touch" on the lot. Once when she went to see her sister, Baby Ruth fell through the floor and had to be hauled out with a crane. Her sister was furious.

Baby Ruth came to a tragic end. While undergoing an operation for a fatty tumor on her thigh, she was taken sick and began vomiting. She was so heavy that she could not turn over on the bed and strangled to death.

Baby Ruth wasn't the only fat person to go through a floor. Johnny Alee, thought by some experts on fatness to be the fattest

Baby Ruth Pontico died in December 1941. She weighed 815 pounds and was married to Joe Pontico who weighed 130 pounds. Her mother was a Ringling Circus fat girl of 600 pounds but her dad weighed only 255 pounds. She is posing with Big Jim, 715 pounds and to her right is Baby Thelma, 655 pounds.

man who ever lived, met his death this way. Just as most midgets and giants refuse to be measured because they exaggerate their height for show purposes, many fat people claim to be heavier than they really are and won't let themselves be weighed. Everyone knew that Johnny was enormous, but since he would not be weighed, no one knew exactly how big he was. Some friends built him a log cabin where he lived by himself. Unfortunately, it was on a slope and one side was propped up with supports. One day his friends came in to find that Johnny had fallen through the floor up to his armpits. He was dead from heart failure. Obviously, he had struggled to pull himself up and his heart couldn't stand the strain. The men managed to get him loose and took the corpse to a weighbridge. They said that Johnny weighed 1,120 pounds, some think a world's record.

Another enormous man was Mills Darden, born in 1799. There is a legend that Mills was abandoned as a baby and adopted by a colored woman who hushed the child by whispering, "Dar den!" to him. It gradually became his name. As she had found him near a watermill, that was used for his first name. Unfortunately, this interesting detail is probably untrue. Mills was almost certainly born in North Carolina (like Johnny Alee), and not only his parents but also his brothers and sisters were well known. His grandson, John W. Darden, who was alive until a few years ago, always denied the foundling story. After living in Texas for some years, Mills finally moved to a farm near the village of Life, about eight miles from Lexington, Tennessee.

Mills was gigantic, but refused to allow himself to be weighed because, although he wasn't in show business, he was sensitive about his size. Some men in Lexington hit on an ingenious idea to determine Mills's weight. Mills rode in an ox cart, the only vehicle that could support his fabulous size, and when he came into Lexington, one man held him in conversation while the others measured the "give" of the cart springs. After Mills left the cart to do his shopping, they filled it up with boulders until the springs registered the same amount of give. The boulders weighed eight hundred pounds. However, Mills kept on getting fatter and fatter and he almost surely weighed well over 1,000 pounds when he died—perhaps more than Johnny Alee.

Mrs Mary Threadgill, who made clothes in Lexington at the time, was commissioned to make a suit for Mills. The coat required thirteen and a half yards of material. The three biggest men in Lexington, weighing over two hundred pounds each, all got into the coat and walked down the street in it.

Mills choked to death in 1857. He developed such huge rolls of fat around his throat that he was unable to breathe. He had been married twice, and had several children.

The fattest man in medical history—that is, the fattest man whose weight was checked by doctors—was Robert Earl Hughes of Fish Hook, Illinois. He weighed 1,069 pounds. He was ten feet four inches around the waist. Robert spent his life in side shows, traveling in a special trailer made to accommodate his vast frame. He lived to be thirty-two years old, getting heavier every year. Then he developed measles. Unable to fit into an ambulance, he was driven in his trailer to Bremen Hospital in Bremen, Indiana, in 1958. He was too big to be gotten into the hospital and, in any case, there were no beds inside that would hold him, so he was treated in his trailer. He developed uremia and died. For a man in his condition, almost any ailment was likely to be fatal. He was buried in Benville Cemetery near Mount Sterling, Illinois, in a piano case instead of a normal coffin. The case had to be lowered into the grave by a crane.

Probably the best-known fat man, at least in modern times, was Happy Jack Eckert. Born in Lafayette, Indiana, in 1877, he entered show business at the age of ten; it was the only profession open to him, for soon he weighed 739 pounds and could barely waddle. He was especially well known for his belly, which hung down almost to his knees and measured eighty-seven inches. The only thing normal about him was his feet: he wore size nine shoes. He was a great joiner and was the largest Moose, Elk and Woodman on record.

Happy Jack was surprisingly healthy for a fat man. He reached the comparatively advanced age of sixty-two without developing any of the usual ailments that affect fat people. While he was playing in Alabama, he was involved in an automobile accident and succumbed to internal injuries.

Women have never reached the enormous growths of men, but the "fat lady" is even a more traditional figure in the side show than the fat man. Possibly the biggest woman who ever lived was a Negress who died in Baltimore, in 1888, and weighed 850 pounds. Close to her was Flora Mae Jackson (Baby Flo), who weighed 840 pounds and died in 1965. As far as I know, the fattest modern woman is Captivatin' Liza, also a Negress, who is said to weigh seven hundred pounds and have a 118-inch bust.

There are several fat people with shows scattered around the country. One is Harold (Big John) Spohn, billed as weighing 809 pounds. He is married to a very attractive woman who is both an albino and a sword-swallower. They work together. Recently, Whitey Sutton, who runs the side show with the James Strates Shows, told me he had a young boy who joined the show and weighed 650 pounds. "He was fine while he was with the show, as we're all used to fat people and know their problems," Whitey explained. "But he went to visit his family and had a fall. He's still suffering from it. I hope he gets well and can rejoin the show, as he liked it here and we all liked him."

I only knew one fat person personally. Her name was Jolly Daisy and she was billed as weighing 750 pounds. Actually, she weighed 690.

We had been having a hard time that season. It had rained on most weekends and been unseasonably cold, and the farmers were too worried about their crops to go to a carnival. Worst of all, we didn't have a freak for the ten-in-one. I was doing sword-swallowing and fire-eating; Captain Billy, the tattooed man, did the Bed of Pain (lying on a spiked board and letting people breaks rocks on his chest with a sledge hammer); Krinko (who ran the ten-in-one) did the block head routine (driving nails up his nose). We had a cowboy who did a whip-cracking routine, a Human Ostrich who swallowed and regurgitated live mice, and a magician. It was the sort of show anyone would enjoy, but we badly needed a freak.

Then one afternoon I ran into Krinko coming around the corner of the cook shack. Krinko was an East Indian and it took a little practice to understand his accent. After doing his act in side shows for forty years, he had finally saved up enough to buy his own show. This was his first season. Everything had gone wrong, and the poor old fellow was half crazy with fear that his show would close and he'd lose everything.

"Now I got good news," he assured me.

"Tonight we get new act. Real freak. Pick up whole show."

I couldn't believe it, because you don't just pick up a real freak halfway through the season. "Who is it?" I asked doubtfully.

"She fat woman, name Jolly Daisy. She with rag show [a cheap carnival] that fold on lot in next town. I go get her tonight."

Well, it wasn't like having the original Siamese twins, but it was a lot better than nothing. Sometimes a fat woman can even make it as a single-O in a small carnival, just the woman sitting inside while a "grind" man at the ticket box keeps repeating the same spiel over and over.

"Do you want to borrow my car?" I asked. I knew that Krinko didn't have a car.

"No, she no can get in a car. I take truck tonight. I marry her first."

"You what!"

"I marry her. She mad at man who has show she with now. She say she not work for any man she not married to. So we get married and elope in pickup truck."

"Is she under contract to him?"

"Yes, but his show close. The man [owner of the carnival] won't take his top [tent] along when they jump [make their next move]. All his acts leave him but not Daisy. She too fat to move. He leave her in top while he drive 'round try to make contact with other show somewhere. Top bad. Sidewalls torn and it rains in on her. She say if I get truck to take her away, she go tonight while he's out."

"You want me to go with you and help?"

"No, I take Paul." (He was our canvasman.) "He know how to drive truck."

I slept on the inside platform that was built along one end of our side-show top. It must have been close to midnight when I awoke suddenly. The top was full of moving shadows and low voices. I heard Krinko's low rumble and Paul's soft voice and knew they must be back.

I jumped off the platform, scratching my head and sides. As I looked around, the sidewall was lifted from the outside and Paul slipped in. He tied the canvas up to a sidepole, leaving a triangular-shaped opening. Through this came the fat woman, staggering and gripping Krinko to steady herself. She looked enormous, and the fluffy pink dress she wore was soaked

Robert Earl Hughes died in 1945 at the weight of 1,069 pounds.

through with sweat. Her thick legs, only partially covered by socks, were barely able to support the great mass of her body swaying uncertainly above them. Her fat baby's face looked around despairingly, as if seeking to drop her bulk somewhere.

"Where's the bed?" she gasped, her breath wheezing in her overtaxed lungs. "Fer God's sake, leave me lie down."

"Right here, lady," called Paul. She stared at him with shortsighted eyes, running a spongy hand through her blonde hair and automatically adjusting her hair ribbon.

"There's the thamned bed!" grunted Krinko. "Hey, son, give a hand here."

Supported by the three of us, Daisy staggered across the top and collapsed onto the bed. Instantly, all four legs disappeared into the soft earth. The fat woman lay there, a mountain of exhausted flesh covered with pink silk. Her dress had ridden high up on her vast thighs, revealing great folds of white lace panties.

"Oh, God, I think I'm dying!" she moaned. Perspiration was trickling off her nose and the ends of her fingers. She had only lain on the bed a few seconds and already it was wringing wet. "I'm dying this time for sure. Oh, I wish I was dead!"

"Give me some help with this bed," panted Paul. "Get some bricks or boards to put under the legs 'fore it goes clean down to the ground."

Krinko and I went to his aid. We tried to lift the cot's legs out of the ground and did manage to get one leg high enough to slip a board under it, but while we were struggling with the next, the board cracked and the leg plunged into the earth again.

"To hell with it," groaned Krinko who was exhausted from straining to lift the seven-hundred-pound bed. "Let the thamned cot sink. Put boards under when she gets up."

Paul brought over a bucket of water and put it by the head of the cot. "You start givin' her drinks, but take it easy or she'll flounder herself," he instructed. "I'll go take them planks outa the truck we used to hoist her in. I'll leave 'em here by the bed where they'll be handy."

Daisy appeared with us in the side-show pit the next evening. She had the catwalk next to mine and we began a conversation. At intervals all evening, Montmorency, the show's talker, would shout in to us from his stand on the platform in front of the top "Bally!" Then, half a dozen of us would troop out with a few props, mount the platform and give a brief show, while Montmorency shouted through the P.A. system and collected a crowd. I passed up one of these ballies, and as Daisy naturally couldn't go, she and I were the only two in the pit and we began talking.

"How do you like married life?" I asked her.

She shrugged contemptuously. "Oh, I been married lots of times before. That old Krinko, he ain't really my husband, an old man like him! That's just what you'd call a business arrangement. Let me tell you, I never had no trouble getting men. Yes sir, that's right," she continued, as I must have looked slightly incredulous. "I've lived with any number of men, although we wasn't always married exactly. But I ain't goin' to do it no more."

"How's that?" I asked.

She shrugged. "Men ain't no good," she said wistfully. "I'd be a good, faithful wife to a decent man but what I figure is a man oughta support hisself some of the time. Not always, of course. A wife oughta help her husband some. But sometimes he oughta make some money for hisself. The last man I had was an awful nice feller, real good lookin', but he always wanted money. Finally I had a fight with him and he blew." She said this somewhat regretfully. "He's the father of my little girl."

"You have a child?" I asked, surprised. "Is she...?" I hesitated, not knowing how to put it.

"Oh, no," said the fat woman without anger. Obviously, she had often been asked the same question. "She ain't fat like me. She's perfectly normal." Reaching inside the great bosom of her dress, she pulled out the picture of a very pretty, curly-headed girl. "This is her," she said, showing it to me proudly. "She's at a Catholic convent. She doesn't know I'm her mother," the woman went on sadly. "It ain't wise she should. But the sisters send me pictures of her all the time. This is the last one they sent me."

The bally broke up as Montmorency turned the tip. Krinko came hurriedly stamping in and ducked under the pit chain. Although crowds could hardly understand him, the old man insisted on acting as the inside talker and introducing the acts.

Daisy eyed him contemptuously as he clumsily adjusted his turban and robe. "That old man ain't no talker." Most of us didn't mind Krinko's blundering efforts as MC, although a good talker can point up an act nicely. We all did our own talking and our acts carried themselves. But Daisy had no act and needed a build-up. "Now that man I was livin' with before his show broke up—the one I left to come here—he was real good. He used to get fifteen minutes o' comedy outa me. He'd do tricks like droppin' a coin in front of me and then sayin' I could have it if I'd stoop over and pick it up. When I stoop over, my skirts ride up so high it shows my bottom and gives the crowd a laugh. Or he'd tell the tip I'd marry any man who could hold me on his lap for five minutes. That Krinko, he jest says, 'This is Jolly Daisy, the fattest woman in the world' and the tip looks and

passes on."

Bronko, the cowboy, had a young fellow named Cal who acted as his assistant in the whip-cracking act. We had picked up Cal in the South while the carny was playing there and he had hung on. His job was to hold out pleated sheets of *The Billboard*, then the outdoor showman's magazine, so Bronko could cut them with his whip. As a climax to the act, Bronko snapped a cigarette from Cal's lips. Sometimes he missed and sliced the end of the boy's nose. Cal never seemed to mind this, but it upset Daisy. At first, she only grumbled and complained, but then she took to shouting out from her seat, "There! You done hit him again! Don't you do that no more, you injun! I ain't goin' to stand fer it!"

One evening after the set, Bronko sauntered past us while the fuming Cal coiled up the whips. Daisy called him over.

"You're too nice a boy to stand there and let that injun or whatever he is cut you up." Her voice softened. "You come 'round to my top after the show and I'll put somethin' on it fer you." The huge woman suddenly became coy. "One o' these days you'll want to take up with a girl and you don't want to be all cut up."

"Oh, I got a girl now," said Cal easily. "I'm married. My wife is only fourteen." He said this proudly, looking around for applause.

"Where is she?" I asked incredulously.

"Back down South. She don't know where I am."

"Then she won't worry," Daisy said soothingly. "But you don't want to go back to her without no nose. You come 'round tonight and I'll fix it fer you."

After that, Daisy became Cal's champion. I had to hold the papers for Bronko, but we omitted the cigarette part. Cal really had nothing to do around the lot; still, since Daisy had put the ten-in-one back in the black, no one said anything.

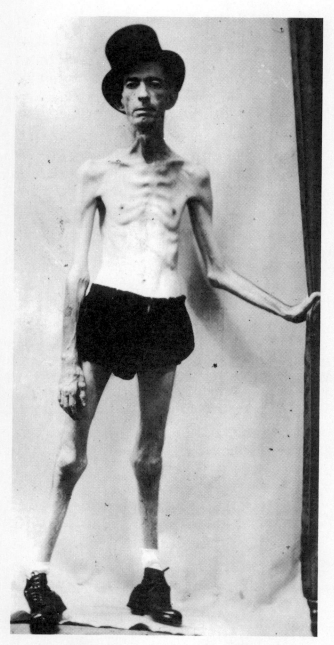

Slim Jim Milton Malone in 1941. He had not been able to gain or lose an ounce since he was attacked by scarlet fever at the age of eight. For the intervening 53 years he weighed 68 pounds, although he had grown to be 5 feet, 6½ inches.

One day Daisy confided to me, "Cal is terrible fond of children. I seen him playin' ball with some of the towny kids that come on the lot in the afternoon. He'd make a great father for a kid on account of he's not

too old and can fool around with children hisself."

"He seems sort of young," I objected. "And he's married already."

"Oh, that don't count. What he really needs is an older woman to look after him some."

About a month later, we were getting ready for the evening show when Krinko came in, followed by a brisk, bespectacled man who was leading a gawky young girl by the hand. She was thin as a sidepole and was wearing a dress so short it ended several inches above her knobby knees. Krinko pointed to Cal and said, "There he is."

Cal looked up carelessly and then stared at the girl in surprise, but without any trace of dismay.

"Hi, Bet," he said. "How'd you get here?"

"This man brung me," said the girl indifferently. She didn't pay any attention to Cal. She was staring in frank amazement at Jolly Daisy.

The man with the spectacles said with professional heartiness, "Well, Betsy, aren't you glad to see your husband?"

Betsy didn't answer. She had just seen Captain Billy, who was sitting on a bed of nails stripped to the waist. "What's that stuff all over him?" she demanded.

"That's tattooing. It won't come off," Cal explained eagerly. "And that's Bronko, who does the whip act, and the Ostrich, who can swallow live rats."

"Come, come," said the man with the glasses a little testily. "This is all very interesting, son, but don't you want to go back to your wife? You have a lovely little baby daughter."

"Do I have to go?" Cal said slowly.

Jolly Daisy broke in. "Sure you gotta go, Cal," she said sadly but a little angrily. "You got a kid to support. What's the matter with you, ain't you got no feeling fer your own kid?"

Cal had an idea. "Say, couldn't you send Bet my wages and let me work here for nothin'? I don't need no money. I can sleep in one of the trucks and the guy at the cook shack'll always give me stuff to eat that he was goin' to throw away. It won't do me no good to go back. I ain't got no money to give Bet."

Jolly Daisy sighed. Then she felt in her vast bosom and came up with a little bag. She pulled its drawstrings and reluctantly produced a small roll of bills, counting out half of them.

"Here, you take this," she said, holding them out to the boy. "You take this and buy somethin' nice fer the baby. Don't you go running away no more. It ain't right. This money'll keep you fer a while."

"Why, I think that's wonderful!" said the Welfare man with artificial enthusiasm. "Aren't you going to thank the lady?"

"Thanks," said Cal, taking the money reluctantly. "But I sure wish I could stay with the show."

Daisy rose without comment and waddled off to the top where she lived. She was still there when Montmorency turned the first tip and Krinko sent me to get her. I found her sitting with damp eyes, dabbing at her face with a little handkerchief.

"I'm glad I found out about Cal when I did," she told me. "I wouldn't want to have nothin' to do with somebody who didn't have no more natural feelings than to run off and leave his own baby. I'm certainly surprised at that boy. I didn't think he was like that."

"As you say, it was lucky you found out in time," I agreed.

Jolly Daisy sighed. "I could of taken him away from her. You saw that for

yourself. He didn't want to go back to her. He wanted to stay here with me. But I'll never take a man away from his woman. A woman done that to me once. It's an awful mean trick and I swore then that I'd never steal another woman's man."

Daisy stayed with us until the end of the season. Then she left to spend the winter in a dime museum in one of the big cities.

Just as midgets are always worried about growing, fat people are worried

Claude Seurat, the French "Living Skeleton" who lived in the early part of the last century.

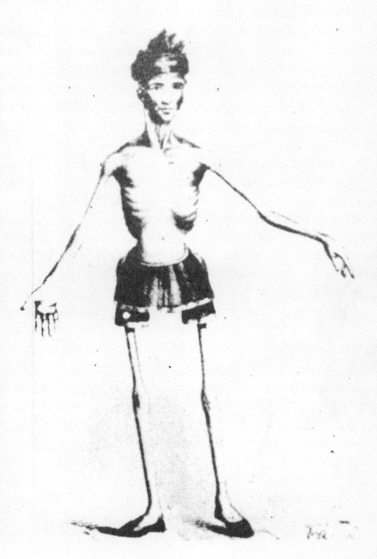

about losing weight; the fatter they are the more of an asset they become. Anyone inclined to plumpness will be glad to know that fat people, even though they are not in show business, have at last rebelled against the ridicule they have had to endure so long and founded the National Association to Aid Fat Americans (or NAAFA for short). They are demanding equal rights for fat people, trying to get legislation passed making it a criminal offense to discriminate against hiring fat people and outlawing jokes about them. The secretary of the society, Mrs Lisabeth Fisher, who herself is only 260 pounds, feels strongly that the days when fat people were a standing joke are nearly over. However, there are still problems. She points out that some states are passing laws making the use of seat belts in cars obligatory, but many fat people can't fasten them because the auto companies don't make belts large enough for them to use. Most firms refuse to hire fat people because of their appearance. "Right now, it's a lot easier to get a black person a job than a fat person," Mrs Fisher says bitterly. She stresses that fat people have trouble traveling on public transportation, finding clothes to fit them, getting beds large enough, and even eating in restaurants because people stare at them and children often openly laugh at them. They have enough problems without job discrimination.

In extreme cases where an individual's life is endangered, it is possible to have an operation to lose weight. Sections of the small intestine are removed, so much of the food eaten passes through the body undigested. Besides the operation itself being dangerous, many fat people have difficulty with anesthetics. The amount of an anesthetic used is computed by body weight.

Since a fat person's heart is no bigger than that of an ordinary individual, he may not survive the large dosage of anesthesia required for an operation. Another difficulty is that too often fat people think that as a result of the operation they can eat anything. This is far from the case. As so much of the food is wasted, they must stick to a special diet to keep them healthy. They cannot drink liquor and virtually must live on yogurt and have bowel movements every two hours or so. Generally, a surgeon refuses to perform the operation unless the individual is at least two hundred pounds overweight and in critical condition.

The opposite of the fat person is the "living skeleton." The most famous was Claude Seurat, a Frenchman who lived in the early part of the last century. I have been unable to find out what he weighed, but he was so thin that his skeleton was plainly visible. You could see his heart beating. He was less than three inches thick. He only ate a penny roll and drank a small glass of wine each day. Although in good health, he was extremely weak. Eddie Masher, billed as the Skeleton Dude, was a well-known figure in circuses during the 1920s. He died in 1962 at the age of seventy. He was five feet seven inches tall and weighed thirty-eight pounds. Harry Jones, born in Lebanon, Missouri in 1860 weighed forty-nine pounds. Dolly Regan, the "ossified girl," knew Percy Pape, who weighed seventy-one pounds. In fact they were married, although Dolly admits this was just a publicity stunt. They were, of course, called the World's Strangest Married Couple.

Skinny people have never been as popular in side shows as fat people. I suppose it's because they're not "funny."

8 The Wild People

From Romulus and Remus to Tarzan, people have been intrigued by the idea of feral children. Perhaps it is some atavistic tendency in us or perhaps it's the same desire to return to the primitive that so charmed Rousseau. In any case, from the earliest times "wild men" have been a standard attraction in side shows.

To the best of my knowledge, there is no such thing as a feral child raised by wild animals. I could be wrong. Lucien Malson in his book, *Les Enfants Sauvages*, lists fifty-three apparently authentic cases of feral children since 1344 who were supposedly raised by everything from wolves, panthers, bears, leopards, monkeys, and gazelles to ostriches. George Gould and Walter Pyle in their monumental work, *Anomalies and Curiosities of Medicine*, give a number of examples of children raised by wolves (mostly in India) which the authors are convinced to be genuine. I still don't believe it. Even granted that a female wild animal would suckle a human child, her milk is so different from human milk I doubt that the child could survive. If it did, the animal would go dry long before the child was weaned. True, wolves and some other animals will regurgitate half-digested food for their cubs, but I can't imagine a child living on this. Certainly, gazelles and ostriches don't do it. Lastly, it is common practice for an animal mother to drive away her last year's litter when she becomes pregnant again for the following year. A human baby would have to be fed for a number of years.

The most authentic case of "wolf children" was the little boy and girl who were

A typical wild man, George Stall was born in Kansas. He was not very mentally bright. His fingernails grew to be 5½ inches. This photo was taken in 1898.

Clicko, the wild African bushman captured by Captain Hepston. This photo was taken in 1930 when Clicko did African dances with the Ringling Bros. Circus.

other one and a half years old. Reverend Singh named them Kamala and Amala. Both ran on their elbows and knees, howled like wolves and preferred offal to ordinary food. Neither could talk. The Reverend Singh took them to Balrampur Hospital at Lucknow, where they lived for several years. Dr Arnold Gesell, director of the Yale Clinic of Child Development, wrote a book on the children called *Wolf Child and Human Child* (Harper & Bros., New York, 1941), and the Reverend Singh kept a diary of the children's behavior. Unfortunately, they both died young: Amala in 1921 and Kamala in 1929. Skeptics have claimed that the children were simply mentally retarded youngsters (often they are unable to walk and must crawl) who had been abandoned by their parents. They also point out that the area where they were found was used as a dump by villagers, which would have supplied food for the children. They claim that there was no proven connection between the children and the wolves who came to the dump as scavengers and had no interest in the two little girls.

In 1940, a baboon boy turned up in South Africa. He was apparently living with a band of baboons. However, it was definitely proven that Lukas (as he was called) was a feeble-minded child and liked to play with baboons, who simply ignored him. Then, in 1946, a gazelle boy turned up in Syria. He was about twelve and, according to accounts, could run on all fours as fast as his foster parents. He was also found to be a feeble-minded boy from a nearby village who would wander away and play near the gazelles, who took no notice of him. An enterprising journalist, sent to Syria to do

found by the Reverend J.A.L. Singh in Midnapore, India, in 1920. The children were said to have been raised by a female wolf and were found near a pair of wolves. They were both girls, one about eight and the

an article on the boy, staged a race with him. The journalist won easily, as the boy could only crawl.

In 1947, a Frenchman named Claude Arrnen published a book on a gazelle boy he found in the Spanish Sahara. The boy could run so fast on all fours that some Americans who hired a fleet of helicopters with trailing nets could not catch up with him. I wouldn't say that Arrnen is a liar, but neither would I say that he misses that appellation by much.

Apparently, there have been races of people who had tails three or four inches long. The Niam-Niams, in Central Africa, were said to have had small tails. Dr Hubsch saw some in the slave market of Constantinople, where they attracted a great deal of attention. In Rajpootana, the rulers had a dynasty of tailed people. Like "lobster-clawed" people, who have hands resembling a lobster's claw, the condition was inheritable.

Although the "wild people" shown in side shows are always advertised as having been captured in the depths of the jungle or raised by wild beasts, their looks are the result of various ailments, just as with all freaks. Perhaps the best known are the hairy people—a condition known as hypertrichosis. In extreme cases, the individual is completely covered with hair anywhere from two to six inches long. Even the forehead is hairy and tufts grow from the ears. This condition is also inheritable, at least in some cases. In the sixteenth century, there was a family named Gonzalis living on the Canary Islands who made a profession out of being hairy. The head of the clan, Peter Gonzalis, was sent to Henry II of France, who treasured him. The family, who until then had been avoided by their neighbors as "devil's children," started farming themselves out to various rulers. Whenever a normal child turned up

among the Gonzalises, it was a family tragedy. Unfortunately, they couldn't find enough hairy people with which to intermarry, so the strain finally died out and future Gonzalises had to work for a living.

Probably the best known hairy woman was Krao, who played side shows in the early part of this century and was described as Darwin's Missing Link. She was—naturally—captured in Africa after a terrific struggle during which she massacred ten tough seamen. (Actually, she

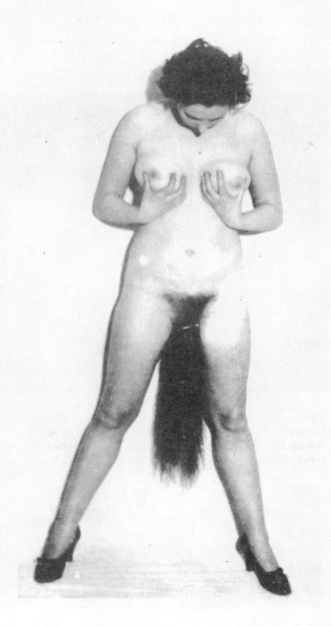

was Siamese and very mild-mannered.) At that time, a number of scientists really took this nonsense seriously and wrote learned treatises on Krao, describing her simian features which existed only in the scientists' imagination. Except for her hair, Krao was a perfectly normal woman. She was intelligent, spoke several languages and liked reading. She continued in show business until her death in 1926.

Today, the only hypertrichosic person I know of is Percilla Bejano, "the monkey-woman." For years, Percilla worked with a pet chimpanzee, Joanna, "her only friend" (except, of course, for her husband and two children). Incidentally, Percilla has a beautiful speaking voice, soft and melodious. I have read several references to the lovely voices hypertrichosic people possess. It seems to be tied in with the condition.

Somewhat distinct from this ailment is the "bearded woman" who, like a man, has a full beard but no hair on her body. Although we generally think of beards as being peculiarly masculine, bearded women are distinctly feminine. If they wished, they could shave and appear normal, although some would have to shave every few hours. Estella, a bearded woman, exhibited herself until she had enough money to go through college. Afterwards, she shaved, became an accountant and married. To avoid attracting attention when she leaves the lot, Percilla

Percilla Bejano, "The Monkey Woman," had a beautiful speaking voice, soft and melodious, which seems to be a symptom of hypertrichosis (excessive hair).

Lionel, "The Lion-Faced Boy" as he appeared in 1907 with Barnum. He was 27 years old, 5 feet 7 inches tall, with hair that completely covered his body and face. A Russian by birth, his real name was Stephen Bilgraski. He claimed that his condition was due to prenatal influence—his mother had seen his father torn to pieces by a lion in front of her eyes while she was pregnant.

Jo-Jo, "The Dog-faced Boy," also a Russian.

tried dressing like a man. "It didn't work," she told me regretfully. "My walk is so feminine that I attracted more attention that way than the other." Some bearded women who shaved later regretted it. Ward Hall told me of a bearded woman with his show who fell in love with a man who ran the merry-go-round. He reciprocated her attention and the lovesick lady shaved to make herself more attractive, whereupon the man lost all interest in her. "It ruined her act, too," Hall complained,

"because it takes months to grow a nice beard like the one she had."

A very famous hairy man was Jo-Jo, the dog-faced boy who looked more like a Skye terrier than do most Skye terriers. He, along with his father, was captured by hunters after a Homeric struggle in Russia's Kostroma forest. His father proved too fierce to be domesticated, but Jo-Jo, being only a child, was more amenable. Both the boy and his father were hairy (this part is probably true as hypertrichosis runs in families). The boy was brought to London by Charles Reynolds, a circus impresario, in 1884. Jo-Jo was five feet eight inches tall and was completely covered with long hair. His real name was Fedor Jeftichew. He was brought to this country by Barnum and soon became one of his star attractions. Jo-Jo was a mild-mannered, quite intelligent young man who spoke several languages. The only trouble Barnum had was getting him to bark and growl at the audience as a dog-man should. Jo-Jo considered such behavior rude.

Old circus buffs probably remember Lionel, the lion-man, who played for many years with Barnum and Bailey. He was a Pole named Stephen Bilgraski. I remember him well in the 1920s. He may have been the hairiest man in history. There wasn't a single spot on his body that was not covered with long hair. Lionel's appearance was due to the fact that his mother, while pregnant, had seen his father torn to pieces by a lion, and the unborn child was marked by prenatal impression. At least, that's what the talker at Barnum and Bailey's side show claimed, and I've never known a side-show talker to mislead the public! Lionel was still performing in the 1930s.

In addition to the hairy ones, who—today, at least—are seldom shown as "wild people," there are the "true" wild men. At one time, there were occasional cases of children or adolescents found wandering in the forests who were captured and exhibited. They were often so misshapen that they had difficulty standing erect. Without question, they were mentally defective children who had been abandoned by their parents to run wild. The most famous of these wild men (he made an important contribution to medical science) was the Wild Boy of Aveyron. In 1799, hunters in the Aveyron Forest of France saw running

ahead of them a strange creature, "four-footed, hairy and mute," which their dogs brought down. The catch proved to be a boy of about twelve. The hunters brought him back and sold him to a showman who exhibited him in Paris.

A young doctor named Jean Itard saw the boy. He was seemingly a hopeless imbecile, naked and dirty, who spent most of his time rocking back and forth on his heels, his eyes unfocused. Itard decided to see what he could do with the poor youngster. He purchased the boy and took him home.

The child did indeed seem more animal than human. He never walked normally—always running either on all fours or bent over. He was unable to sit in a chair. He smelled everything handed to him before touching it. Many of his actions were completely incomprehensible. When given a dead canary, he expertly plucked it, opened it with his nails, smelled its insides—and dropped it. He would ignore a pistol fired over his head, but jump when a walnut was cracked. Snuff did not make him sneeze and he could pick potatoes from boiling water. Dr Itard, working slowly and with infinite patience, was able at last to train him to perform simple tasks. Gradually he won his confidence.

Then Itard tried a cruel experiment, because "I wanted to find out if he was indeed an animal or capable of telling right from wrong." The doctor had occasionally punished the boy for various faults, and the child had accepted the punishments without resentment. Now Itard deliberately punished the boy unjustly. Subsequently he wrote in his scientific report, "The boy rushed at me, bit me, then ran and hid in a closet, weeping bitterly. I also wept at my own cruelty."

After two years, the once-wild creature was "an almost normal child although he never learned to speak." He could, however, read a few words, was clean, affectionate and well-mannered. He lived to about the age of forty.

With this experience, Itard later trained a Doctor Séguin, who put his knowledge to such good use in helping the mentally retarded that he became known as the "apostle of the idiot." Séguin's work, in turn, strongly influenced Maria Montessori, who pioneered progressive educational methods.

Perhaps the most famous wild men were the "Wild Men of Borneo," called Waino and Plutano. Actually, they came from Connecticut. Only slightly larger than midgets, they were feeble-minded, but exceptionally strong. They could pick up a six-foot man easily. Plutano died in May, 1907 at the age of eighty-seven, and Waino died in March, 1905 at eighty, so show business did not seem to affect their health.

Somewhat similar were the "Aztec Children." They were Indian children from Central America and also feeble-minded. Professor Owen made an extensive study of them. They had a mental age of about two years but were lively and curious and could speak a few words. In 1867, it was announced that they had married, but this was almost surely a publicity stunt since they were probably brother and sister—although it was claimed they were from a strange tribe living deep in the jungle.

Eko and Iko, the "sheep-headed men," had to be seen to be believed. They were ambassadors from Mars, discovered in the Mojave Desert near the remains of their spaceship. An alternate theory was that they were albino Negroes named Willie and George from Louisiana. But if you

believe a wild story like that, you'll believe anything. Joseph Hilton, who handled them for a time, says they weren't very bright. They had a mania for eating and used to steal extra food from the table and hide it under their coats. Then they'd pile it under their chairs on the platform and eat during the show. Their conduct would probably be explained by the fact that there isn't much food on Mars. Hilton recalls that when the show was playing Los Angeles, the boys had saved up enough money for either a woman or a new suit of clothes and couldn't decide which they wanted more. They debated this important

The Aztec Children, pinheads for the Barnum Circus.

Unidentified pinhead with movie stars Rochelle Hudson and Chester Morris.

issue for three days. Hilton doesn't remember what they finally decided.

A real wild man was Fiji Jim, who did indeed come from the Fiji Islands and was named Ruto Semm. Ruto was highly successful in show business, but he was homesick and carefully saved every cent he made so he could return to his beloved islands and retire there for life. A few days before he managed to accumulate the necessary sum, he was playing at Rockaway Beach and saw a swimmer drowning. Ruto promptly dove into the rough water and rescued the man. He contracted pneumonia and died a few weeks later.

In any discussion of wild people, some reference should be made to geeks, although they are not truly freaks. Geeks were made famous by William Lindsay Gresham in his carnival classic, *Nightmare Alley.* A geek sits in a pit wearing some outlandish costume and kills chickens and snakes with his teeth, afterwards eating them raw. It's not an act that appeals to everyone, and Gresham claimed that geeks were always alcoholics who were driven to this life in return for an unlimited amount of booze. This, however, is not always true. Still, I think it would be fair to say that geeks rank at the bottom of side show attractions. There was only one famous geek, Bosco, who specialized in eating live snakes. The talker's cry of "Bosco, Bosco, eats 'em alive!" was a popular catchword at the turn of the century. Bosco was before my time, so I never caught his act. I have only seen two geeks: one was a woman and obviously feeble-minded; the other, a man who gave up geeking to do the Ladder of Swords (walking up a ladder made of sword blades in his bare feet).

To the best of my knowledge, there are no geeks showing today. Audiences wouldn't stand for it, to say nothing of the SPCA. Geeks are always advertised as wild people who insist on eating their food raw and alive. Even among geeks there is a hierarchy. A "glomming geek" seizes his prey with his hands and tears it apart. An ordinary geek is so drunk or feeble-minded that the animals have to be put into his mouth. Glomming geeks consider themselves far superior to ordinary geeks.

The largest group of wild people is the pinheads. Pinheads suffer from a condition called microcephaly and have heads that come to a point, somewhat like an old-fashioned dunce cap. They are born this way and it seems to run in certain families. There is no cure for it. Pinheads are always mentally retarded—the only group of freaks who are—and have to be cared for like infants. Sometimes a parent or relative travels with them. Sometimes they are virtually adopted by showmen, because their families don't want them and institutions find them a nuisance. They are always advertised as belonging to some wild tribe somewhere or other and are frequently dressed in skins.

Some showmen get along well with pinheads and others find them a problem. I suppose a good deal depends on the pinhead and on the showman. Joseph Hilton recalls one pinhead girl he exhibited who had such a low mentality that she couldn't even recognize her own mother. She would grab cotton candy from children as they walked past her platform, and her chair had to be chained to the catwalk to keep her from falling over. "She was really hard to handle," Hilton recalls, "but she was a great attraction. As long as her parents were paid, they didn't care what became of her."

Ward Hall has more pleasant memories of them. "I always found them very lovable," he assured me. "Like little children, they become completely dependent upon you, and it is a great shock for them to be separated from someone to whom they've become attached. They need a great deal of attention and, if they don't get it, become quite morose. Usually everyone with the show plays with them to keep them amused. They learn to look forward to the tip's applause and laughter and, if they don't get it, are greatly upset. It's their whole lives."

Hall recalled the case of Schlitzie, a well-known pinhead who played in the motion picture, *Freaks*. Schlitzie was somewhat more intelligent than most pinheads and could obey simple commands. He was really a man, but always dressed as a woman because it was easier to take care of his toilet needs if he wore skirts. He had a sister who was also a pinhead. Schlitzie was in show business for thirty years and then his manager—or to be more explicit about it, his owner—died. The side show wanted to keep Schlitzie, but the state insisted on putting him in an institution. What happened was exactly what occurred to Sally, the pinhead I knew. Sam Alexander, who now runs a side show in Montreal, Canada, went to see him and found poor Schlitzie literally dying of loneliness. The attendants in the mental institution were far too busy to pay any attention to him and Schlitzie was pining away. Alexander managed to persuade the authorities to release Schlitzie to him, and once again Schlitzie was happily on the road. He lived to be eighty, dying in California.

I have said that all pinheads are mentally deficient, but some, like little children, have the knack of saying clever things. One such pinhead was Zip, the Missing Link, who died in 1926 at the age of eighty-four—the grand old man of side shows. Zip was one of P.T. Barnum's finds and, by shrewd showmanship, Barnum made him famous. Side-show buffs are still arguing whether Zip was an idiot or a very clever actor playing the part of an idiot. Unlike many pinheads, Zip could talk easily and well. He was, of course, captured in Africa and wore a sort of union suit covered with fur. To accentuate his pointed skull, Barnum had his head shaved except for a tuft of hair at the top—a procedure now standard for all pinheads. Actually, Zip was an American Negro.

Zip had one famous stunt. Occasionally, someone in the tip would throw him a coin as they might to an organ grinder's monkey. Zip always threw the coin back! This was accepted as clear proof that Zip was crazy, and people used to attend the show just to toss coins at Zip and get them flung back. The idea was that Zip was too stupid to realize the value of money. According to the story, someone with the show finally asked Zip why he didn't keep the coins. Zip retorted, "Because if I did, they'd stop throwing them."

Zip wasn't so crazy that he didn't manage to accumulate a comfortable little fortune, which is more than plenty of show people have done. At last, in his old age, he retired to a farm in New Jersey. It is said that on his deathbed he smiled at an old circus crony and said, "Well, I sure fooled 'em for a long time."

Anton LaVey, who has had many years' experience with freaks, always liked pinheads. "They're the only people I know who are completely happy. They don't worry and have nothing to worry *with*. The ones I knew craved affection. Like children,

they loved to dress up. I knew only one pinhead who wasn't an idiot. His name was Ickey and I'd describe him as having the mentality of a shrewd kid of ten or eleven. Ickey didn't belong to any show, but specialized in conventions. He'd turn up with a big button on his coat reading 'ASK ME' and show the delegates around. I don't know how he lived; mainly, I'd say, on handouts and tips. I saw him around for many years and then he disappeared."

By far, the most famous pinhead of all time was Triboulet, court jester of Francis I of France during the early part of the sixteenth century. Triboulet's life inspired Victor Hugo's famous play *Le Roi s'amuse* and forms the basis of Verdi's immortal *Rigoletto*, one of the best-loved of all operas. Triboulet's head came to such a sharp point that he wore half an orange peel as a cap. A contemporary of his observed: "His bowed back, short and twisted legs, and long dangling arms amused the ladies, who regarded him as though he were a monkey." He also had enormous ears.

It is difficult to say just how intelligent Triboulet was. As with all famous jesters, many of the clever sayings attributed to him may have been old jokes or actually uttered by other people. Most of his witticisms Triboulet probably didn't mean to be funny; they were just said with simple honesty. And, naturally, he went in for the crude horseplay typical of all early jesters.

Triboulet was a native of Blois, and had been jester to Francis while the latter was Count of Angoulême. In 1515 when Francis became king, he took Triboulet along with him. The courtiers were jealous of the freak's supposed influence over the weak, dissipated monarch, and Triboulet revenged himself by making jokes at the nobles' expense. Once when Francis was handing out awards to notables, the king asked at the conclusion of the ceremony, "Now, is there anything else I can do to show how France feels toward these great men?" Triboulet said contemptuously, "Yes, hang the bastards!" One of the nobles furiously turned on the jester and shouted, "I'll cut your throat for that, you scoundrel!" Francis promptly told the angry lord, "I'll have your head cut off ten minutes after you kill Triboulet." Triboulet interposed anxiously, "Excuse me, cousin Francis, but couldn't you arrange to do it ten minutes before?"

Yet the king's favor was not always able to protect Triboulet from the victims of his practical jokes. There was the time he slit the seat of a young noble's breeches so neatly that the young man didn't realize what had happened until his bare bottom started popping out as he bowed to the ladies. That evening, the nobleman, together with some friends, waylaid Triboulet as he was leaving the palace. The terrified jester was dragged to the town gibbet and nailed to it by his big ears. Triboulet was nearly dead when he was found next morning. The furious king called up all the lords Triboulet accused of having taken part in the plot, but none would confess. At last, the king told his jester, "I've cross-questioned everyone and they all deny being there that evening." Triboulet replied bitterly, "Well, that leaves only me and I promise you I didn't nail down my own ears."

Not even the king was safe from Triboulet's jokes. Once during a dinner when the king had drunk far too much wine, he grew tired of the jester's sneers and said angrily, "Remember our relationship, fool!" Triboulet retorted, "I remember it well. I'm a better man than you on two counts: I'm not king and I'm not drunk." The king burst out laughing and Triboulet was saved.

So many stories are told of Triboulet that it is impossible now to separate truth from legend. According to a widely believed tale, Francis became enamored of the beautiful young Diana de Poitiers, daughter of the aristocratic Count de Saint-Villiera. Francis kidnapped the girl and seduced her. Her outraged father denounced the king before the entire court. Triboulet mimicked the heartbroken old man's gestures behind his back while the court howled with laughter. When the count turned around and found out what was going on, he laid this curse on the jester: "May you suffer as I do." The story says the curse was fulfilled when the courtiers, to avenge themselves on the jester, kidnapped his own daughter and turned her over to the king. Triboulet died of grief. It is on this legend that Hugo, and later Verdi, based their works. If Triboulet was able to father a child, he was a very unusual pinhead. Most have no sexual capacities.

Although pinheads are still exhibited, wild people are growing increasingly rare in side shows. Nobody believes in them anymore. The world is becoming too well known. Until recently, I never encountered a medical term that embraced all the various types of freaks who are exhibited under the general title of "wild people." Then a young woman who works in a children's hospital told me there is such a term. From time to time, a doctor would come up from the delivery room and remark casually to his colleagues, "There's an FLK in room B. You ought to take a look at it." My friend spent a long time wondering what FLK meant. "It sounded so technical," she explained to me. Finally, she broke down and asked a doctor. He looked at her in surprise and said, "Why, don't you know? It means Funny-Looking Kid."

9

What Does It Feel Like to Be a Freak?

Obviously, no one can really answer this question except a freak, and even then it would depend on the temperament of the individual and the type of deformity. Emmett, the "alligator-skinned man," can pass unnoticed as long as he is fully clothed, since his ichthyosis has not spread to his hands and face. His wife Percilla, on the other hand, has long hair that covers her face and is sure to attract attention unless she wears a veil. Midgets and dwarfs are sure to be noticed, but at least they can

Lucy Elvira Jones, shown here at age 13 at the Texas State Fair in 1894. She was double-jointed at the wrists and elbows and ran around on all fours like a dog.

move about easily, while fat and tall people have trouble walking. All these factors affect a freak's attitude toward his condition. Another is a freak's emotional reaction to his state. Some freaks regard their deformity as a "meal ticket" and would not want to be normal. Percilla is often asked, "Why don't you shave, so you'd look like other women?" Her answer is, "If I did, I'd be down in the tip with the rest of you instead of standing here on a platform making a good living."

Some take great pride in being different, such as Frank Lentini who, as a "star," considered himself vastly superior to ordinary side-show acts like fire-eaters and sword-swallowers. Anton LaVey, who spent many years in circuses and got to know a large number of freaks intimately, told me that Lentini, when he was fishing and using his third leg as a stool, used to enjoy the astonished double-takes of the people who passed him. "Curiously enough, although Frank was proud of his third leg, he was extremely sensitive about an extra thumb he had growing from his knee," LaVey recalls. "He always took pains to keep it covered and was annoyed if anyone mentioned it." To Lentini, the thumb constituted a deformity and he was ashamed of it.

Some freaks make a joke of their deformity, such as the Siamese Twins Chang and Eng giving the conductor one ticket and daring him to put the other off the train. To still others, like Edward Mordake who killed himself rather than live with his "devil twin," their deformity is such a fearful curse they cannot endure it.

Observers, too, may react differently to various types of freaks. The midgets whom I have known, like Meinhardt Raabe, Buddie Thompson and the Del Rios, struck me as extremely nice people. Anton LaVey admits that he never got on well with midgets, although he never had any prob-

lems with dwarfs and today has several good friends who are dwarfs. I should say something here about LaVey, who is a most remarkable man. After leaving show business, he founded the Church of Satan in San Francisco, a growing concern that has attracted nationwide interest. As I understand the basic tenets of the group, it regards Satan as the friend, rather than the enemy, of mankind who introduced Adam and Eve to the Fruit of Knowledge; he is looked upon as the god of rebels against unjust authority. LaVey tells me a number of freaks have joined his sect, "because

This man is Robert Milwin, billed as an Australian. He was at the Trenton State Fair in 1954. I never heard or saw him again. He could have been a grift (a fake) but I don't think so since I've never seen anything like this before or since, and don't know of any reference to such a deformity.

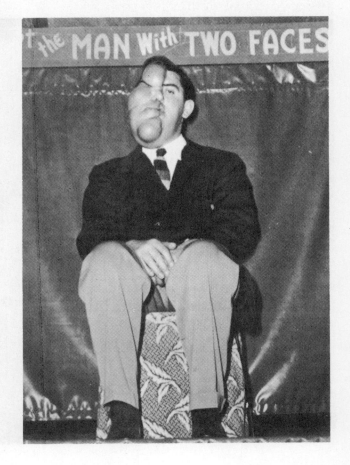

they feel that God has treated them unfairly by allowing them to be born deformed, and Satan, himself an outcast, has more sympathy for their plight." LaVey's interest in freaks has led him to purchase the all but forgotten classic film *Freaks* by Tod Browning and re-release it. It has proven so popular that it has created a cult, even though television has refused to touch it.

"In my experience, midget men tend to be unsure of themselves," LaVey explained. "They have baby faces and high voices. To compensate, they often smoke the biggest cigars they can find and run around with the flashiest, biggest blondes. I remember once on a circus lot seeing a midget trying to move an elephant tub (one of the big tubs elephants stand on during their act). I went over and offered to help him as I would anyone having difficulties. He turned and cursed me out. That's typical of most of them; they are so sensitive about their size it's an obsession. Dwarfs, although deformed, have deep voices and adult faces. They seem to accept their position and don't try to pretend that they're normal."

Bodin and Hersh in their study of midgets, *It's a Small World*, come to the same conclusion as LaVey, but Buddie Thompson, himself a midget, wrote to me, "Those two damn fools didn't know anything about us and that book is enough to make any midget's blood boil." I merely mention this to show how observers can get opposing impressions. However, it is

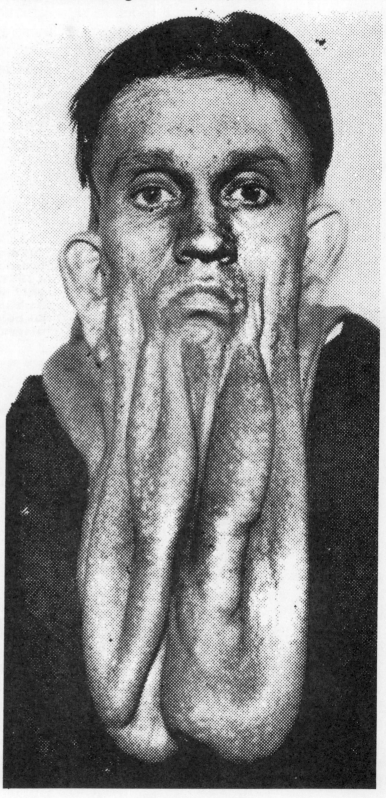

Arthur Loose, the rubber-skinned man with his neck stretched down at least eight inches due to a skin disease. This was taken at the "Believe It Or Not!" show at the Chicago World's Fair, 1933.

only natural that small men would try to compensate for their height in various ways, such as being attracted to large women. Prince Arthur, a black midget with Whitey Sutton and in show business since 1948 (he is now sixty-four years old), is married to a woman who weighs 264 pounds. Although Prince Arthur is only thirty-four inches tall, it has been a most happy marriage.

It would be a great mistake to think that all freaks have psychological problems. Ward Hall told me, "I have always had more trouble with actors—and especially with actresses—than with freaks." In a letter to me Jon Friday, side-show manager with the Sells & Gray Circus, warns, "Freaks vary from individual to individual as greatly as all human beings, and it would be unkind and foolish to describe them all as being dependent and childish as others have done. You must understand that several famous freaks have been feeble-minded [such as pinheads]; others are at the genius level. Some are happy, many are unhappy with their fate."

My feeling is that the great majority of freaks have adjusted. Although they might be unhappy in the outside world, they have found a niche for themselves in show business where they can be among their own kind or with people who understand them. Gibsonton, Florida, is an example of how they can create a world of their own without being molested by unsympathetic people.

Anyone who thinks that freaks must be emotionally disturbed should meet Dolly Regan, the "ossified girl." Although few human oddities have it worse than Dolly (she suffers from ankylosis of the joints and muscular dystrophy, which have the illusion of turning her body into stone), she is a tiny ball of energy—being only about three feet high—and an excellent talker

with a great sense of humor. Unable to walk or even to stand, with the use of only two or three fingers she buzzes around her little cottage in Gibsonton in her electric wheelchair like a whirligig beetle on a mill pond. Dolly isn't the only ossified person on record; P.T. Barnum exhibited the famous J.R. Bass for many years until one day during a fire an attendant who was carrying Bass to safety dropped him and he *broke*. Unlike Jeanie Tomaini, who finds that running her restaurant and motel occupies all her time, Dolly is active in civic affairs and has a number of cups and plaques presented to her by the grateful community.

"I was born in Canada fifty-six years ago," she explained to me while darting around the room in her powered wheelchair. She was giving last minute directions to friends and neighbors' children who had come in to help her pack, for she and her husband, Scott, were leaving in a few days for Milwaukee. "My parents were always worried about me because they didn't want to see me put into an institution or become a burden to my brother after they died, and yet what could I do to earn a living? Well, when I was twenty-three I was selling tickets for an exhibition playing under the auspices of the Kiwanis Club when the manager of the side show saw me. I'll bet he was never so glad to see a girl like me, since he'd recently lost three acts and his show was getting ready to fold. He offered me fifty dollars a week—a regular fortune! But at the same time I was terrified. I'd never even seen a side show, let alone been in one. I was completely tied to my wheelchair and someone had to push me; they didn't have electric chairs in those days. When I was wheeled into the side-show top, it wasn't only my body that was ossified—it was my mind, too. But the carnies were so friendly I soon got over my fright. I remember Sealo especially [Sealo had flippers like a seal instead of hands]. He acted as a big brother to me and showed me the ropes. That evening, a man asked me for a date. It was the first time anyone had ever wanted to date me. I nearly cried.

"I was really a Johnny-come-lately then. I remember when I first met Grace McDaniels, the 'mule-faced woman,' I

Grace McDaniels, the so-called mule-faced woman, in 1947. While she is perhaps the homeliest woman in the world she is happily married and the mother of a fine son.

fainted. Of course, I felt terribly badly about it later as Grace was the kindliest person in the world."

There was some excuse for Dolly. Harry Lewiston in his autobiography, *Freak Show Man*, gives the following description of Grace:

"Her flesh was like red, raw meat; her huge chin was twisted at such a distorted angle she could hardly move her jaws. Her teeth were jagged and sharp, her nose was large and crooked. The objects that made her look most like a mule were her huge, mule-like lips. Her eyes stared grotesquely in their deep-set sockets. All in all, she was a sickening, horrible sight."*

Grace got into show business by winning an ugly woman contest. Rather surprisingly, she was married and had a son. The marriage was a happy one and the boy was devoted to his mother. He became her business manager. Grace had trouble speaking because of her deformed mouth, but was always so pleasant and cheerful that she was welcome everywhere.

Dolly has been married three times; her first two husbands died. "She has so much energy she wore them out," remarked Mr Scott, her present husband, somewhat bitterly. In her thirty-three years of show business, Dolly has met most of the great freaks, such as the Hilton sisters ("a little stiff but nice"), Mary Casey and Benny Rogers, who had both male and female organs; and Serpentina, who was born in Douglas, Ontario, and had no bones in her body except in her head and neck. "She was really remarkable," recalls Dolly. "She could bend every part of her body. Bill Gregory took care of her, for of course she was absolutely helpless. I remember she didn't trust banks and put all her money into diamonds. She was pleasant and smiling."

* From *Freak Show Man*, copyright 1963. Published by Holloway House Publishing Co., Los Angeles, Calif.

Dolly agrees with Joseph Hilton and Ward Hall that there is still a tremendous interest in freaks. "When Ripley put on his Believe It or Not! exhibition, he was losing thousands of dollars a week, because all he had were articles of various types. Then 'Cash' Miller took it over for a percentage of the take. Cash promptly introduced live freaks and, in a short time, Ripley was making a profit of thousands of dollars a week."

I asked Dolly if she thought most freaks felt rejected by their parents. "Not freaks in show business. Parents who reject a deformed baby put it in an institution right away. If they keep the child, it means they love it—perhaps more than they would a normal child. In fact, many freaks are rather spoiled as children; their parents do too much for them."

Dolly is now appearing in Ward Hall's side show with Goodings' Million Dollar Midway. She travels during the summer months and winters in her comfortable house in Gibsonton.

A couple who have adjusted extremely well to their way of life are Emmett and Percilla Bejano. They have been in show business for nearly fifty years, Emmett since he was four years old. Both were adopted by showmen and have no complaints. They have two children, a girl going to college and a younger boy who travels with them during the summer. Both could pass as normal people, Percilla by shaving and Emmett by taking care to always keep his body covered; but as Emmett remarked, "Why punch a meal ticket full of holes?" Emmett, incidentally, possesses virtually total recall. I had met

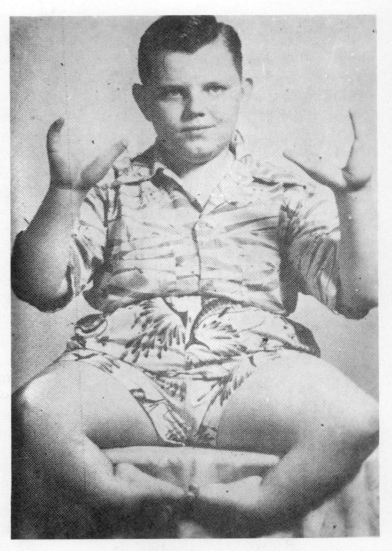

Grady Styles, "The Lobster Boy," whose family has passed this trait on for five generations.

them briefly with the Johnny J. Jones Shows on a lot in Washington, D.C., in 1942. When I walked into the ten-in-one this spring in Philadelphia, Emmett not only instantly recognized me, but told me the exact date and place of our first meeting. Whitey Sutton considers the couple the greatest sideshow attraction in America today and the second greatest in history (he puts only Betty Lou Williams above them).

Anton LaVey told me that two of the best-adjusted people he has ever known were freaks. One was Johnny Eck, whose real name was John Eckert. Johnny was a half man. Born without legs, he walked on his hands. He had a twin brother who was normal and entered the Navy. Johnny was an accomplished musician, played the piano and organized his own orchestra. He

Johnny Eck, born without a body below the waist, has a normal twin brother. Being without legs, he walks on his hands. Johnny is an excellent pianist and when not on tour with the circus, he has his own orchestra in his home town of Baltimore, where he is well-known. Johnny is also an accomplished painter.

was also a wonderful gymnast. He played in several motion pictures, including *Freaks*. "Johnny was extremely intelligent, always good-natured and one of the best people to be with I've ever known," LaVey recalls. "There are very few normal people I have such a high regard for."

Some freaks are extremely proud of their deformities, such as Frank Lentini of his third leg. The Styles family have been "lobster people" for five generations; that is to say, their fingers are fused together so they resemble a lobster's claw. "It's no wonder they're proud of it," Joseph Hilton remarked somewhat resentfully. "It's made them a fortune. Grady Styles and his daughter ran a single-O with one carny where I had the side-show concession and they did better than I did with ten acts. Grady thinks the world of his daughter; if she had been normal, it would have broken his heart. He shows himself first and then charges extra to bring her out. The Styles aren't as unique as some freaks I've seen, but the public loves them."

Some types of freakiness runs in families: a tendency to produce midgets or pinheads, fatness and a few others. As with the Styles family, a group so distinguished may consider a blessing what others would regard as a curse. Apparently, ichthyosis—alligator skin in showman's lingo—is found not only in families but in certain districts.

Joseph Hilton told me: "Most of the best alligator-skinned people come from North Carolina. I don't know why and I've never heard the chamber of commerce boast about it, but that's been my experience. We were showing in North Carolina one season when a boy in his late teens walked into the ten-in-one and asked, 'Can you use me?' I certainly could. He was the best alligator-skinned person I'd ever seen. Even his face and hands were covered with

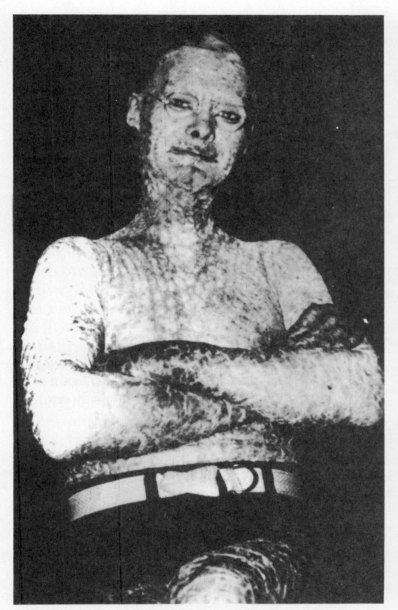

John H. Williams, an alligator-skinned man, was born in Elwood, Indiana and went to school with Wendell Wilkie as a child. He is married to a bearded lady.

father wanted five hundred dollars. I told him that was too much and asked for my hundred dollars back, but he refused. I was stuck.

"I had an idea and went to the home of the man he sharecropped for. This man lived in a fine house full of black servants and received me very pleasantly. It turned out he was an old circus and carny buff and was willing to help me. We drove to the sharecropper's shack and he asked the man, 'Did you take this fellow's money and promise to let your son go with him?' The cropper had to admit he had. I told the father I'd send him twenty-five dollars a week as long as the boy worked for me, and he said, 'Why the hell didn't you tell me that before? I thought I was selling the kid to you outright.' The owner said to the boy, 'Get your clothes,' and the boy dashed into the house and came back with a cardboard box with a few things in it.

"We got in the car, but before we drove off I saw someone playing peek-a-boo 'round the door with me. The boy said casually, 'That's my sister. She's even worst than I am.' Believe me, I didn't lose any time jumping out of that car and running to the shack. The girl was a little older than the boy, and he'd told the truth when he'd said she was worse than he was. She was simply covered with scales. I asked her if she wanted to make fifty dollars a week and she nearly cried, she was so excited. She'd have come with me for nothing—she was so eager to get away from that place.

"We were starting back to the car when the old mother rushed out. 'What do you mean, tryin' to steal both my kids?' she

scales. He had so many of them that some would flake off and fall to the ground. Since he was under twenty-one, I had to get his parents' consent, so we drove to his house, a dirty little cabin owned by a sharecropper. Well, the father asked me for a hundred dollars which I gave him and arranged to come back the next day to get the boy. I came back all right, but now the

These are two elephant-skinned children of Ciudad, Mexico. They were brother and sister—one of the rare times when normal parents have given birth to consecutive freaks. The photo was taken in 1930 when Rose was 9 and Paul was 11. They are now deceased.

ent,' she said. 'How much?' I paid them another hundred for the girl and we took off.

"Those kids were a sensation. I paid them fifty dollars a week and they sold little Bibles on the side, so they averaged anywhere from ninety to a hundred dollars a week. They slept in a trailer and once a week I had a man go in there and sweep out the scales they'd shed. The inside of the trailer looked as though someone had been throwing corn flakes around. For a time, we didn't have a cook house with the show and I couldn't get the children into a restaurant. People were afraid of them. Then I thought of explaining they'd been badly burned in a fire. After that, everything was all right.

"The girl was as nice and gentle a person as you'd want to meet. She was everlastingly grateful to me for getting her away from that shack. Fred Smythe [from Ringling Brothers and Barnum and Bailey] went to her and offered her double the money she was getting from me, but she turned him down. She said she wouldn't leave me in the lurch halfway through the season. Later, she married and now has ten children, all normal. It's a pity, but that's how things work out sometimes.

"The boy was a little devil. He was always into something. I remember a drunk turned up on the lot, a fellow they called Toto; he was a real wino. I don't think he had brains enough even to geek. The boy virtually adopted him and took care of him like a baby—or a pet dog. He traveled everywhere with us until one night he got too much bootleg liquor in him and died. The boy was heartbroken. He insisted on

screamed and went at me with a broom. It was all I could do to hold her off until the father came out and hollered, 'Woman, he's *payin'* us for the kids!' 'Oh, that's differ-

before we left town. I gave him the undertaker's address and he went there and started wandering about the place. He opened the wrong door and walked up to a group of mourners sitting around a coffin and asked, 'Am I in the right place?' Those mourners took one look at him and went flying out of there; door or windows—it didn't matter to them. The undertaker was furious and wanted to call the fuzz, but I talked him out of it. The kid thought it was

William Durks was married to Mildred, an alligator-skinned woman. He had two noses and two eyes (the center eye is painted on).

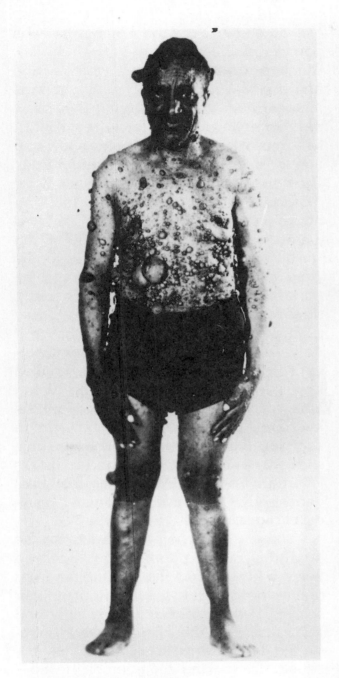

"The Knotty Man," 1947.

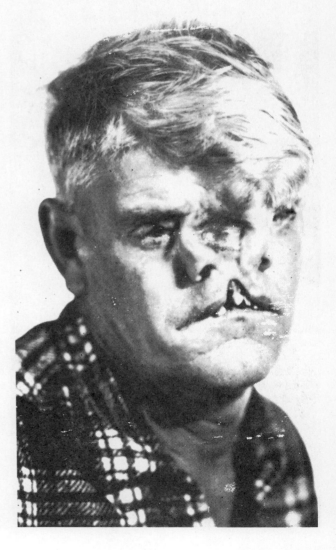

giving Toto a decent burial instead of just turning him over to the morgue. I saw an undertaker and made all the arrangements. The undertaker got Toto all fixed up and put him in a coffin for the viewing, although there were no mourners. I told the boy about it and he insisted on seeing Toto

such a big joke he forgot all about Toto. He loved to scare people."

Several freaks have shown a certain grim humor about their appearance. Bill Durks was such a one. Bill was advertised as "the man with three eyes." He had two noses and a harelip, and gave the illusion of having three eyes. As Bill is now dead, it can do no harm to say that his middle

Pop-eye Perry, who had the ability to pop his eyes out of their sockets.

eye—the one between his noses—was painted on. Bill was married to Mildred D. Durks, an alligator-skinned woman. She had lived with her family until she was middle-aged, when apparently they grew tired of her and she was forced to go out on her own. She met Bill in the side show and they were married a few months later. They were with Whitey Sutton's show for eighteen years. "A very devoted and happy couple," Whitey recalls. Mildred died a few years ago and Bill this spring [1975]. When Bill had to leave the lot, he wore a large cap with a big brim which he pulled down over his face. Occasionally, some idiot—the type who feels it's his duty to interfere with anyone out of the ordinary—would go over to Bill and ask sneeringly, "How come you got that cap pulled down over your face? Something wrong with you or what?" Bill would avoid the heckler as long as he could but if the man kept it up, Bill would walk over close to him, suddenly pull the cap back and thrust his face right up close. "Most times, they faint dead away," Bill would recall with considerable satisfaction.

Another freak who enjoyed scaring the daylights out of people was Pop-eyed Perry, a black man who had the amazing ability to pop his eyes clean out of their sockets. It was a bloodcurdling sight and Perry knew it. After the talker had introduced him, Perry would select some squeamish-looking member of the tip—usually a woman—and, thrusting his face toward her, suddenly pop out one of his eyes. The lady usually screamed and reeled back. Then Perry would pop out the other eye. Not infrequently, this was enough to make the girl faint. Perry would wait until she had recovered and then, bending over her, pop out both eyes at the same time. Invariably, this was enough to knock the woman out a second time.

Sealo, the "Seal Boy," named for his flipper-like arms, in 1932.

Of all the human oddities, I think the most impressive are the armless ones. Although not as amazing as freaks, the incredible way these people can use their feet as hands is wonderful. Watching the ease and skill they display, every member of the tip feels a certain awe and respect for them. I remember watching Frances O'Conner (who was with the Cole Brothers circus for many years) cut her food with a knife and fork held in her toes, uncork a bottle and pour herself a drink, and then as a finale load and fire a gun at a target. She never missed. After watching her for a few minutes, you forgot she was using her toes; her movements were so natural that she seemed to have hands. Frances told me that when she ate in a restaurant, the other diners seldom noticed that she was eating with her feet.

Another remarkable performer with no arms is Sealo. His hands grow directly from his shoulders. In addition, his fingers are fused together, so they resemble the flippers of a seal. This condition is known medically as phocomelia. In his act, Sealo shaved himself, signed his pictures and sawed a board. About the only thing he couldn't do was close the zippers on his trousers, and he solved that by using a stick with a hook on the end. Sealo proudly showed me a letter he had received from a priest asking for his picture. The priest worked with handicapped people and wanted to show them Sealo's picture to illustrate how a man apparently hopelessly handicapped can overcome difficulties. "I believe it will be an inspiration to them," the good father concluded. Sealo is now retired and living in a home for aging showmen near Gibsonton. I talked to many people who remember when he was a star attraction, and all spoke of his unfailing good nature and cheerful disposition.

A famous team for many years was Eli Bowen (legless) and Charlie Tripp (armless). They used to ride a special bicycle together, Eli doing the steering and Charlie the pedaling. They had a favorite gag. At intervals, Charlie would shout in pretended anger to his partner, "Watch your step, can't you?" to which Eli would retort, "Keep your hands off me!" In addition, Tripp was an excellent carpenter—and could have made his living that way—while Bowen was an accomplished acrobat.

I must admit that not all armless people have been paragons of virtue. In 1579, an armless man was hanged in England—for cheating at cards. In this country during the last century, there was an armless man arrested for highway robbery. I can only say these two individuals showed a lot of

The legless man is Eli Bowen, whose feet grew out of his hips, and the armless man is Charlie B. Tripp, 1897.

enterprise.

If armless and legless people demand respect, I don't even know what words to use for people who have neither arms nor legs. I had the pleasure of working for a short time with Frieda Pushnik, who was a human torso. Frieda was born in 1923 with only tiny stumps for hands and no legs at all. She could sew, crochet, put on her make-up and type—all by using her stumps, which were only a couple of inches long. Her mother and sister traveled with her and took care of her. She weighed thirty-eight pounds.

Another remarkable "human torso" was Prince Randian, a Negro said to have been born in the West Indies. I never saw Randian, but Anton LaVey knew him well: LaVey told me, "I would put him with Johnny Eck as one of the finest people I have ever known. There was a dignity

about him I'll never forget. He was married and his wife was devoted to him as well she might have been. Randian's most remarkable stunt was to roll and light a cigarette with his lips."

The outside talker always introduced Randian as the "human caterpillar who crawls on his belly like a reptile!" Randian was able to move by wiggling along the ground on his belly. He appeared in the motion picture *Freaks*, and I recall one magnificent scene at night when Randian, illuminated by flashes of lightning, writhes across the mud of a circus lot with a knife held between his teeth toward the beautiful blonde seductress who had betrayed his midget friend. It was a real bloodcurdler.

Ward Hall told me of Emmett (no relation to Emmett Bejano), also armless and legless, who appeared in his show. Emmett once told Hall that as a child, his father would put out his clothes for him but strictly forbade anyone to help dress the boy. "I thought he was being cruel, but now I'm grateful to him," Emmett had related. Emmett is a remarkably skilled mechanic, and whenever anything breaks down on the lot, Emmett is sent for. He operates his tools with his mouth. Ordinarily, Emmett finds it difficult to move, but Ward Hall recalls that once during a tornado, with the twister bearing down on him, Emmett by a miracle not only went flying out of the tent but actually into the truck. "He just bounced along on his behind," Ward remembered. "I don't know how he did it and probably neither does he."

There is a French human torso named Pierre Mahieux who published a brief autobiography that makes frightening reading. When he was born and his mother saw him, she died of shock. All through his childhood his father kept saying, "Why did God do this to me?" At school, the children

Eli Bowen

Frances O'Connor was born armless in 1917. She taught herself to do everything with her feet, including holding a gun with one foot and pulling the trigger with the other.

at first laughed at him, but later adopted him as a sort of mascot. Two of the biggest boys served as his personal attendants and carried him everywhere. "I only learned then that children are not really cruel, only curious," he wrote. Pierre became very fond of children and used to make them toys, manipulating the tools with his lips. Once when he was alone in the cottage where he lived with his father, a hot coal leaped out of the grate and fell on some papers which caught fire. While the helpless boy watched, the flames spread to the walls and he realized he was going to be burned alive. At the last moment, his cousin happened to come in and save him. "God must have sent her," Pierre believes.

Unlike Randian and Emmett, Pierre was apparently unable to move at all. During the First World War, nearly all the villagers in the community where he lived fled as the German Army approached. Pierre found himself deserted. To make matters worse, packs of famished dogs invaded the village, killing and eating everything they could find. Pierre remembers lying on the ground in front of his home, watching them approach and giving himself up for lost. Again he was miraculously saved—this

Prince Randian, the human torso, was born without arms and legs. He does everything with his mouth and can even roll a home-made cigarette with his sensitive lips. He was happily married and his wife was devoted to him.

time by a passerby.

There are three types of freaks I have never seen nor, as far as I know, has anyone who is alive today. One is a *sirenomelus*, or mermaid. In this condition, the legs are fused together so the individual appears to be standing on a pedestal. Ambroise Paré describes one who was born in Ravenna in 1512. Even rarer is the Cyclopean freak, a person with one eye in the middle of the forehead. A little girl was born like this in Tourcoing, France, in 1793. She lived to be fifteen. A few years ago, it was rumored that there was a Cyclopean Negro living in Mississippi. One enterprising showman is said to have spent months and a small fortune trying to find him, without success. The third is a condition called by the impressive name of *acardius acephalus*, in which the face appears to be on the chest. Apparently, this condition occurred more frequently in medieval times or it especially appealed to the old artists, for they were fond of portraying it in woodcuts and believed that there were whole communities of such people living in India or Africa. I have never even seen a photograph of such a person.

So far, I have emphasized that the vast majority of freaks are either proud of their unique appearance or at least reconciled to it. I believe this to be true. However, there are some tragic exceptions. Such a one was Margarete, Duchess of Tyrol, Princess of Carinthia, one of the richest and most powerful women of the fifteenth century. She may well have been one of the ugliest women who ever lived. Her subjects contemptuously referred to her as "sack-face." Rather than attempt to describe her, I refer the reader to her picture by an unknown artist, in the National Gallery in London. Sir John Tenniel used this painting as a model for the ugly duchess in *Alice in Wonderland*.

In her youth, Margarete tried hard to be a good ruler and was a capable and wise woman. She was married at the age of twelve to another child for political reasons. Later, when her husband betrayed her, she was forced to have him murdered for her own protection. She was again forced to marry for reasons of state and again, after brutal treatment, had her second husband killed. Although she was a kind ruler, her subjects insisted on regarding her as a monster because of her hideous face. She took an albino man for a lover. Since he was also a freak, she hoped he could love her, but was disappointed as he ruthlessly exploited her. She finally retired to a convent where she died. A biography of this tragic woman has been written by Lion Feuchtwanger: *The Ugly Duchess* (Grosset & Dunlap, New York, 1928).

Probably the most terrible freak in history was the elephant-boy who lived in England during the latter half of the last century. Sir Frederick Treves, a society

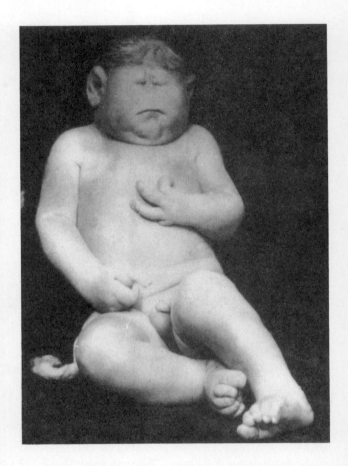

Like most Cyclops babies, this one did not live long after birth.

physician, was called out of bed one night by a dirty, itinerant showman. The man wanted Treves to treat a sick boy. The doctor followed him to a bare, ice-cold garret. In one corner crouched a boy, trying to keep warm by covering himself with a pile of rags. Treves describes him:

"He had a fleshy appendage hanging down from his forehead like an elephant's trunk. A spongy growth covered his neck. He was completely hairless. His forehead covered one eye. A mass of bone from the roof of his mouth projected out from his upper jaw. He had no nose. His body was hung with sacks of wrinkled skin. His right hand resembled a fin. His feet were too swollen to allow him to walk except by a shuffling gait. In addition, he had been dropped when a baby and his backbone was twisted out of shape."*

The showman had bought the boy from his parents and was trying to exhibit him. The police closed the show, and since the showman was broke, he'd been unable to get lodgings. Treves gave him some money, and the man took the freak to France. Again, the police closed him down and the showman simply abandoned the boy.

The poor freak managed to exhibit himself long enough to get money for his return passage. When he appeared in public, he covered himself with a long robe and wore a mask, somewhat like a Ku Klux Klan getup. This outfit attracted nearly as much attention as his natural appearance.

When Treves saw him again, the boy was crouched in a gutter, weeping bitterly and trying to shield himself from a laughing crowd which was pulling at his robe to get a better look at him. Treves took the boy home and wrote such a bitter account of the child's misfortune that the elephant-boy became a society fad. Wealthy people visited Treves' apartment to see the boy and always left a substantial sum for his support. Although the good doctor never thought of it, he was actually running a high-class blow-off.

The visitors were always careful not to comment on the boy's looks, and after a while the freak began to grow more cheerful and told the doctor that perhaps he wasn't so bad after all. Then one day a nurse, who hadn't been warned about the boy, entered his room by mistake. She fled, screaming. Treves hurried to the boy's room. The boy's face was so deformed he could not register any emotion, but while Treves watched, he saw a big tear roll down the boy's cheek.

Treves sent the boy to a farm where he wouldn't be forced to meet people. The boy could have been happy, but he was determined to be like other people. He always slept in a sitting position, resting his massive head on his knees, until he discovered that ordinary people didn't sleep like that. The boy decided to sleep prone. When he lay down, his heavy head fell back, shutting off the narrow vent through which he breathed. The most terrible freak in history quietly strangled. His story is told by Ashley Montague in *The Elephant Man* (Outerbridge & Dienstfrey, New York, 1971).

No matter how grotesque a freak may be, it is remarkable how quickly you forget about a person's appearance and accept him for what he is. Ward Hall told me, with quiet amusement, about a talker he had who was so disgusted by the looks of some pinheads with the show that he avoided them as much as possible. "I can't understand why anyone would pay money to look at such creatures," he told Hall. A few days later, the same talker said to Hall in astonishment, "Why do people carry on so about the pinheads? I've seen women scream with terror and men turn away in disgust. Why, they're just lovable kids. I don't see anything unusual about them at all."

---

* From *The Elephant Man*, by Sir Frederick Treves, Henry Holt, New York, 1884.

10

How to Be a Freak

"What kind of a question is that?" Whitey Sutton retorted rather irritably when I asked him if he thought freaks liked being freaks. "They're born that way and have no choice."

Of course, he was right, but a surprising number of people have deliberately made themselves into freaks. The first question here is, what is a freak? To Neanderthal man we would appear to be freaks. In Kenya, the natives fled the first white men they saw, thinking the strangers had leprosy. In 1890, Dr Martin Couney, the inventor of the incubator for premature babies, found no institution would put up money for the new device, so he exhibited his "incubator babies" at Coney Island as part of a freak show. He shocked the medical profession, but saved the babies. In 1906, L. Frank Baum wrote *John Dough and the Cherub*. In it John Dough is transported to the mysterious Isle of Phreex where, in addition to meeting fat people, a midget monarch, a double-headed dog and other monstrosities, he encounters a genuine incubator baby which he considers to be as bizarre as the other inhabitants.

In the name of beauty, millions of people have mutilated themselves over the ages. The Flathead Indians of North America constricted their babies' skulls with tight bandages, Chinese women bound their feet until they could scarcely totter along, a Ubangi woman was not considered attractive unless she could fit a butter dish into her lips, the "giraffe-necked" women of Burma stretched their necks with copper wire, the

Leo Konges from Pittsburgh, Pa., is able to pound 40 penny nails into his nose and bend them down with a hammer. His nerves do not register pain at all. He is able to ram hat pins through his flesh, and literally sews on his socks without bleeding or scarring.

Martin Laurello in 1940 at the "Believe It or Not!" show at the New York World's Fair. He has the ability to turn his head completely around so that his chin rests on his spine, as shown. Anyone else attempting to do this would have to break at least two neck vertebrae.

Peruvians used cloths to train their children's heads into points like pinheads and East Africans stretched the lobes of their ears until they reached their shoulders. This list does not even include such comparatively mild customs as facial scars, nose rings, painted faces and filed teeth. A Nile woman urged Lady Baker to get her lover to knock out her front teeth "so she would be beautiful."

Naturally, we would regard these people as savages, but until recently European and American women lashed themselves into such tight corsets to achieve an eighteen-inch waist that their rib cages were permanently distorted. Many men regard tattoos as a sign of virility. We are still uncertain whether long hair on men is a crime against nature or an acceptable custom.

Some of the great beauties of the past were deformed. Diana de Poitiers had one breast higher than the other, and men were charmed by Ruben's voluptuous models who, by today's standards, are fat slobs. King Adolphus Frederick, who ruled Sweden in the eighteenth century, had seven mistresses: two were one-eyed, two were one-legged, and two were one-armed. The last one had no arms at all.

As there have never been enough freaks to supply the demand, almost from the earliest times there have been men skilled in the technique of producing them, just as there have been men trained in the production of dancers, tumblers and other entertainers.

George Ebers, the writer-archaeologist, describes how the ancient Egyptians produced dwarfs by raising a child in a box which would distort his body, or by strapping him on a board with his limbs twisted into weird positions until the bones became fixed. The Romans carried the art of freak-making to great heights. Longinus, in his work *De Sublimibus*, tells of "children called 'nani' who were raised in cages which attenuate them." The joints of children intended as tumblers or contortionists were skillfully dislocated. Etruscan vases have been found in the shape of deformed children. It is thought a baby would be put into such a vase with only his head and legs protruding. His body would then grow into the shape of a vase. Eventually, the vase would be broken and the child sold for a huge sum.

After the fall of Rome, the technique of

making freaks, at least in Europe, became a lost art for over a thousand years. Then, in 1400, Tamerlane swept into India at the head of his wild Mongolian hordes. Many of the people in his way died, more submitted, a few fled. Among those who survived were certain Hindustani tribes who migrated westward to become ancestors of the modern gypsies. These tribes brought with them their ancestral crafts: horse training, fortune-telling, metal working. They also brought along a special caste with another, more peculiar craft: the manufacture of freaks. This caste, lately known as the Dacianos, apparently had its headquarters in Spain. Professor John D. Fitz-Gerald, writing in 1910, remarked that while he was in Spain he visited the Gorge de Pancorbo near Vitoria. "This gorge was once the haunt of 'child-buyers.' Here they had a laboratory where children were mutilated." This group also met near Diekirsch, Germany; Bourbonne-les-Bains, France; and in England at an old square tower near Cleveland, Yorkshire.

Victor Hugo in his famous novel, *The Man Who Laughs*, calls this group the Comprochicos (child-buyers). As far as I can tell, Hugo invented this name, because the group was always known as the Dacianos. Dr Carlos Garcia in his work, *La Desordenada de los Bienos Agenos* (1619), gives this description of them: "The Dacianos kidnap children three or four years old and, breaking their arms and legs, lame and disfigure them so that they may afterwards sell them to beggars, blind men and other vagabonds." Hugo says: "They worked on human beings as the Chinese work on trees . . . they could mark a child as though he were a pocket handkerchief . . . they produced toys for men . . . "

The exact means used to produce deformed children are no longer known in detail. Many of the descriptions that have come down to us of the techniques used betray their origins in pure superstition. The *Miscellanea Curiosa Medica Physica* (1670) says that to make a child into a dwarf "his backbone should be rubbed with the grease of moles, bats and dormice." This treatment would have no effect at all on the child's growth. But even simple people have known of really effective methods. A Dr Clarke, who toured Lapland in 1870, saw mothers feeding babies raw spirits to stunt their growth, and de Maupassant tells of pregnant French women who strapped themselves with corsets so tightly that their children would be born deformed and thus bring a high price from traveling showmen.

Surgery was also used. Astonishingly complicated operations have been done by primitive doctors with crude instruments. Children could be turned into "mermaids" by skinning the inside of their legs and then binding the legs together to graft them, thus producing the effect of a tail. A Dr Macgowan, who practiced in China in the 1880s, described seeing "animal children" who he believed were the result of elaborate surgery. Dealers, he said, kidnapped small children and skinned them alive bit by bit, replacing the human skin with pieces of hide cut from living dogs or bear cubs. The grafting process took months, and when it was completed, the child's vocal cords were cut and his joints disconnected so he was forced to run on all fours. Dr Macgowan was told that only one child in five survived the operation. The odds seem a little high; modern medicine would say such an operation could not succeed, since no way has yet been found to graft skin permanently from one human being to another, let alone from an animal. But perhaps the Chinese specialists knew something our doctors don't.

Macgowan added that the torture of this

operation permanently affected the children's minds so that they were little better than idiots, which is hardly surprising. Simpler operations, however, which could be performed quickly under an anesthetic (both opium and Indian hemp—better known here as marijuana—were used as soporifics in the Middle Ages) would no more damage a child's mind than modern plastic surgery. An old recipe for producing a "laughing mask" called for "cheeks slit clear to the ears, gums laid bare and nose battered." Such a child could be used as a clown with a perpetual grin on his face.

It was not only peasant children who were mutilated. On occasion, the tortuous political intrigues of the Middle Ages required the alteration of a child so that he could not be identified. The child could not be killed, for he might be needed later on as a political pawn—but he must not be recognizable. In 1649, the son of the executed Charles I, who was eventually to become Charles II, had a child by a young girl named Lucy Walters, described as "brown, beautiful and insipid." Charles acknowledged his parenthood, so the queen, his mother, had the baby boy kidnapped. It was suspected that the Dacianos were involved. But even the queen could not have Charles's son killed. In case Charles had no legitimate children, his child of joy would be needed to carry on the bloodline. If legitimate heirs were born, however, then the child must be unidentifiable. The queen's plans failed, for the child was recovered in Holland.

Experts were also needed to castrate young boys, so they could either serve as eunuchs in harems or perform as fantastic singers. These male sopranos, especially common in Italy, were called *castrati* and had a range and volume impossible for women. There still remains in Rome hundreds of musical scores which today no living voice can encompass. Historians say there were four thousand *castrati* in Italy in the seventeenth century. One of the most famous was Farinelli. The half-insane King Philip of Spain could find comfort, even if only temporarily, in the sound of Farinelli's marvelous voice, so the singer lived at the Spanish court, where he was said to have attained more power than anyone else in the kingdom except his patron. The *castrati* continued to sing in churches until 1878, when Pope Leo XII forbade their performances. As late as 1886, it was reported by a Dr Curran that he saw traveling eunuch-makers in India plying their trade for the equivalent of $8.64 an operation.

Another art in great demand during the Middle Ages—and later—was infibulation. In this operation, a ring was passed through the head of the penis. This procedure served the same purpose as castration, but was not permanent. It was usually performed as a punishment. Consequently, as a reward for good behavior, the ring could be removed. A similar operation was performed on girls by passing several rings through the lips of the vagina, thus insuring the girl would remain a virgin. Many Oriental monarchs would not accept a girl for their harems unless she had been infibulated as a baby. The last case of infibulation known in the U.S. occurred in New York in 1894. A woman went to a Dr Collier and complained she was infibulated with a padlock. Her husband carried the key and unlocked her only when he desired sexual relations. She wanted to know if her husband wasn't exceeding his legal rights.

Perhaps the most notable of freak-making operations was that which created "cocks" for the kings of England. For some reason, long ago, it became a tradition in the court to have a human cock who crowed each hour of the night. To produce this combination of rooster-watchman, an operation was performed on the larynx of a child so he could do nothing but crow. At the time of James II, the cock received nine pounds, two shillings and six pence annually. During the reign of Charles II his mistress, the Duchess of Portsmouth, objected so much to the saliva which constantly dripped from the cock's mouth (incessant salivation was one result of the operation) that Charles substituted for the mutilated cock an ordinary man who could imitate the crowing. Even this functionary was finally dropped by George II. When George was Prince of Wales and newly arrived from his childhood home in German Hanover, he was eating supper one evening when the cock crowed just behind him. George jumped a foot, and even the explanation that the cock was an old tradition didn't pacify him. As soon as he became king, he fired the cock.

By the nineteenth century, apparently no trace of the Dacianos remained, but in 1828 in Nuremburg, Germany, there occurred a curious event which has never been satisfactorily explained. On May 23, a cobbler was leaving his shop when he saw a boy of about seventeen leaning against a stone wall. The boy's skin had a strange, waxlike quality and he was shielding his eyes from the sun. The cobbler spoke to him, but the boy could only gibber in reply. He had two letters. One was addressed to the commanding officer of a regiment of dragoons stationed in Nuremberg, suggesting that he make the boy a soldier. The other, supposedly from the boy's mother, said she was unable to support him and gave his name as Kasper Hauser. Handwriting experts later proved that both letters were written by the same person, who had attempted to disguise their common origin.

The cobbler took his find to the dragoon barracks, although the boy proved virtually unable to walk. His legs were bowed, and the soles of his feet were as soft as a baby's. He would eat nothing but bread and water. Sunlight blinded him, but he was able to see in the dark. Later, it was shown that he could make out the stars in the daytime. His sense of smell was so keen he could identify different people by their odors without seeing them.

Kasper was taken into the home of a Professor Daumer, who taught him how to speak. Five months later, the professor published an account of Kasper. The boy claimed he had been brought up in a cellar

Etta Lake has elastic skin and can pull it out at least 6 inches. King and Franklin Circus, 1889.

where he had only a wooden horse as a toy. Bread and water were lowered down to him. One day the water tasted "nasty" and he instantly fell asleep. When he awoke, he was in Nuremberg.

The case of the "Child of Nuremberg" aroused international interest, which Kasper's former jailers had not foreseen. On October 17, 1829, Kasper was discovered lying unconscious in a cellar, his head streaming blood. When he recovered, Kasper said that a man "with a black face" (apparently a mask) had hit him with a club. The attack caused a new sensation. Professor Daumer now felt that Kasper was no longer safe in his home, and the boy was put under the guardianship of Lord Stanhope, a wealthy Englishman who was interested in the case. But before Kasper could be taken to England, he was stabbed, supposedly by the same mysterious assailant. The boy lingered on for two days, then died.

The case of Kasper Hauser is one of the great mysteries of all time. Two investigators (Daumer and Feuerbach) believed that Kasper was the legitimate son of Grand Duke Charles of Baden and that he had been kidnapped at the order of the Countess of Hochberg, the duke's morganatic wife, so that her own son would inherit the title. Other students of the case consider Kasper a fraud who invented the weird tale and stabbed himself to gain sympathy, although the doctor who attended Kasper testified that the knife had been driven through two thicknesses of a padded coat from such an angle that the injury could not possibly have been self-inflicted.

There is a strange sequel to the story. Dr Macgowan, the student of Chinese "animal children," said in 1897 that he had heard of a young boy who was exhibited in Kiangsi province. The lad had curious

waxlike skin, was unable to walk, and could see in the dark. He attracted a great deal of attention and was regarded with superstitious reverence until it was discovered that he had been raised in a cellar by a group of child-buyers for exactly this purpose. The method was a fairly common one for producing this special type of freak. So, perhaps Kasper Hauser was the last of the Daciano children. No one will ever know.

The wretched victims of the Daciano had no choice except to become freaks, but in modern times a number of people have

Agnes Schmidt of Cincinnati, Ohio, the "Rubber-Skinned Girl."

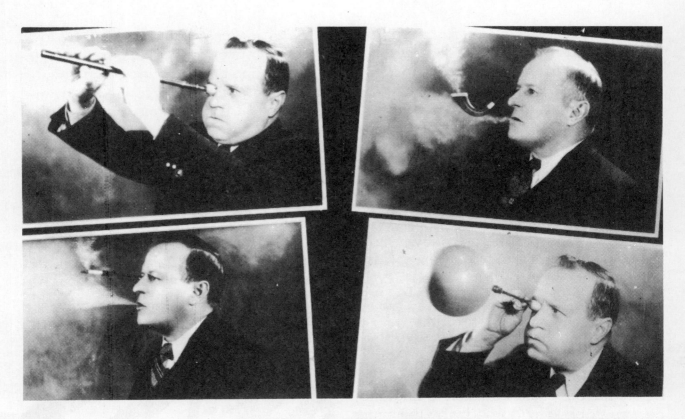

Alfred Langevin was able to smoke, blow soap bubbles and even blow up a balloon through his eyes.

deliberately made themselves into freaks for financial reasons. One of these is Rasmus Nielson, who is completely tattooed from neck to feet and has two great loops of flesh dangling from his chest by which he can lift enormous weights. Nielson worked as a blacksmith in the California mining camps during the end of the last century. Like many miners, he amused himself during the long winters by having designs tattooed on his arms. Finally, he had so much tattoo work that he decided to capitalize on it and have his body covered completely. But he found there were a lot of tattooed men in show business with the same idea so, as an additional flash, he had two metal rings set into his chest. Later, he discovered that by passing a bar through these rings, he could lift weights suspended from it. Continual weight-lifting

finally produced the loops of flesh which made him famous. Nielson attracted nationwide attention when he was able to lift a 20-pound anvil. One day a smart young reporter jumped on Nielson's platform and shouted that the anvil was wood. Nielson told him to pick it up. The reporter struggled vainly to lift the anvil while other newspaper men happily took pictures. The resulting publicity made Nielson one of the best known side-show acts.

One of the most remarkable cases of a man deliberately turning himself into a horrible freak is the great Omi, the Zebra-Man. The Great Omi was reportedly the son of a wealthy, upper-class Englishman and he attended one of the great English public schools. Tall, handsome, and cultivated, he entered the British Army where he became a major. In World War I, he fought with the Desert Mountain Corps in Mesopotamia and was decorated for bravery. After the war, he came into a considerable inheritance which he squandered in riotous living. Trying to re-enter the army, he was rejected, then lost what little money he had left in a farming venture.

Ruined and despondent, he had one last inspiration. His hobby had always been circus life and he knew that freaks often made considerable sums of money. In 1922, the ex-officer went to George Burchett, the famous London tattooer, and asked to have himself completely tattooed from head to foot. The design he chose had nothing to do with the conventional ships and girls; instead, he had his entire body, including his face and even the top of his head, covered with zebra-like stripes one inch wide. The job took 150 hours and required 100 plastic surgery operations because certain areas, such as the eye cavities and the throat, cannot ordinarily be tattooed. The pain of the tattooing was so intense that Burchett was able to do an average of only two inches a day, but at last the work was completed.

As the Great Omi, the former officer has received some of the highest fees paid in

Koo-Koo the "Bird Girl" of Ringling Circus dances (left) while Zip the Pinhead plays a violin and Schlitzie pecks at the piano.

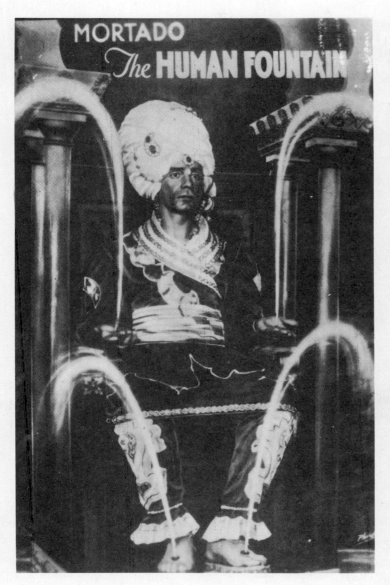

Mortado, "The Human Fountain" at Coney Island, 1930. He had holes bored in his hands and feet, then inserted silver pipes and by means of pressure was able to squirt water through them.

appearance—so he spent the war years exhibiting himself for war charities and making a motion picture for 20th Century Fox. He contributed his salary to the troops.

Another man who went through agonies to become a freak is Mortado. He actually had holes bored through his palms and feet to make it look as though he had been crucified. Afterwards, he was forced to keep wooden plugs in the holes to keep them from growing together. His act consisted of having jets of water squirted through the holes, so that he was billed as the "human fountain." Whitey Sutton told me that Mortado also allowed nails to be driven through the holes, rupturing small sacks filled with a red fluid resembling blood. "People in the audience used to faint when he did it," Whitey assured me. During his last years, Mortado dropped in popularity. Shortly afterwards, I read that a man had been found crucified to a wooden wall of an elevated train station in New York, but when police investigated, they found it was a fraud; the man had crucified himself. As it is impossible to crucify yourself, I have often wondered if this was Mortado making a last bid for fame.

I know of only one woman who deliberately made herself into a freak. This was Koo-Koo, the "bird girl," who appeared with Ringling Brothers for many years and was also featured in the motion picture *Freaks*. Anton LaVey told me, "She was not a freak at all. She was a gangling, homely girl from New York who dressed in special costumes and learned to exaggerate her worst features. She sucked in her cheeks and popped out

European show business. In 1938, he appeared in Ripley's Believe It or Not! show on Broadway, then toured with Ringling Brothers-Barnum and Bailey; he has been exhibited in Madison Square Garden and has traveled all over Europe and America. During World War II, he again tried to re-enlist but was rejected—this time for his

Human Torso from the deep jungles of Africa who crawls on his belly like a rep-tile!" I remember the old Bradenburgh Museum in Philadelphia where for the price of one dime—ten cents—you could see Jo-Jo, the Dog-faced Boy; Plutano and Waino, the Original Wild Men of Borneo; Laloo from India with his twin growing out of his body; Arthur Loose, the Rubber-Skinned Man who pulled out his cheeks eight inches and let them snap back into place; and the famous Mrs Tom Thumb. The popularity of freaks carried the show, but various vaudeville performers, not yet good enough for the Palace or Roxy's in New York, were used as fillers. Among the people who got their start there were Al Jolson, Harry Houdini, Buster Keaton and Van Alsyne, who sang a little number he'd written called "In the Shade of the Old Apple Tree." Though these men did well later on, it was always the freaks whom people came to see.

END.

her eyes to make herself look grotesque. Otherwise, she was a nice, quiet person whom you'd never notice."

I'm sorry to see the passing of the old-time side show with the talker shouting through his mike, "Step closer, ladies and gentlemen. See the World's Greatest Collection of Human Oddities. Randian, the

RE SEARCH

Catalog

RE/Search #14: Incredibly Strange Music Volume I

Enthusiastic, hilarious interviews illuminate the territory of neglected vinyl records (c.1950-1980) ignored by the music criticism establishment. Genres include: outer space exploration; abstract female vocals; tiki "exotica" (featuring bird calls and jungle sounds); motivational (*How to Overcome Discouragement* and *Music to Make Automobiles By*—made for factory workers); promotional (giveaways like *Rhapsody of Steel,* produced by U.S. Steel); lurid stripping and belly dancing (which often included instruction booklets); easy listening; and experimental instrumental (which used Theremin, Ondioline, Moog, whistling, harmonica, sitar, accordion and organ). Lavishly illustrated, with reference sections, quotations, sources and an index, this is a comprehensive guide to the last remaining "garage sale" records. Volume 1 (Volume 2 scheduled for Fall 1993): 8½x11", 208 pp, over 200 photos & illustrations.

$17.99

Featuring:

- ◆ **Eartha Kitt**
- ◆ **The Cramps**
- ◆ **Martin Denny**
- ◆ **Amok Books**
- ◆ **Norton Records**
- ◆ **Perrey & Kingsley**
- ◆ **Mickey McGowan (Unknown Museum)**
- ◆ **Phantom Surfers**
- ◆ **Lypsinka**
- ◆ **Mike Wilkins (author, *Roadside America*)**
- ◆ **and others . . .**

RE/SEARCH BACKLIST

RE/Search #13: Angry Women

Featuring:

- ◆ *Karen Finley*
- ◆ *Annie Sprinkle*
- ◆ *Diamanda Galás*
- ◆ *bell hooks*
- ◆ *Kathy Acker*
- ◆ *Avital Ronell*
- ◆ *Lydia Lunch*
- ◆ *Sapphire*
- ◆ *Susie Bright*
- ◆ *Valie Export*
- ◆ *Wanda Coleman*
- ◆ *Linda Montano*
- ◆ *Holly Hughes*
- ◆ *Suzy Kerr & Dianne Malley* ◆ *Carolee Schneemann*

16 cutting-edge performance artists discuss critical questions such as: How can you have a revolutionary feminism that encompasses wild sex, humor, beauty and spirituality *plus* radical politics? How can you have a powerful movement for social change that's *inclusionary*—not exclusionary? A wide range of topics—from menstruation, masturbation, vibrators, S&M & spanking to racism, failed Utopias and the death of the Sixties—are discussed passionately. Armed with total contempt for dogma, stereotype and cliche, these creative visionaries probe deep into our social foundation of taboos, beliefs and totalitarian linguistic contradictions from whence spring (as well as thwart) our theories, imaginings, behavior and dreams. 8½x11", 240 pp, 135 photos & illustrations.

$18.99

"In this illustrated, interview-format volume, 16 women performance artists animatedly address the volatile issues of male domination, feminism, race and denial. Incendiary opinions of current issues such as the Gulf War and censorship and frequent allusions to empowering art and literature make this an excellent reference source. These informed discussions arm readers verbally, philosophically and behaviorally and provide uncompromising role models for women actively seeking change." —
PUBLISHER'S WEEKLY

"This is hardly the nurturing, Womanist vision espoused in the 1970s. For the most part, these artists have given up waiting for the train of sexual equality . . . The view here is largely prosex, proporn, and prochoice . . . Separatism is out, community in. Sexuality is fluid, spirituality ancient and animist. Art and activism are inseparable from life and being. The body is a creative field, the mind an exercise in liberation. This is the 13th step, beyond AA's 12: a healing rage."
—**THE VILLAGE VOICE**

RE/Search #12: Modern Primitives

An eye-opening, startling investigation of the undercover world of body modifications: tattooing, piercing and scarification. Amazing, explicit photos! *Fakir Musafar* (55-yr-old Silicon Valley ad executive who, since age 14, has practiced every body modification known to man); *Genesis & Paula P-Orridge* describing numerous ritual scarifications and personal, symbolic tattoos; *Ed Hardy* (editor of *Tattootime* and creator of over 10,000 tattoos); *Capt. Don Leslie* (sword-swallower); *Jim Ward* (editor, *Piercing Fans International*); *Anton LaVey* (founder of the Church of Satan); *Lyle Tuttle* (talking about getting tattooed in Samoa); *Raelyn Gallina* (women's piercer) & others talk about body practices that develop identity, sexual sensation and philosophic awareness. This issue spans the spectrum from S&M pain to New Age ecstasy. 22 interviews, 2 essays (including a treatise on Mayan body piercing based on recent findings), quotations, sources/bibliography & index. 8½ x 11", 212 pp, 279 photos & illustrations.

$17.99

"**MODERN PRIMITIVES** is not some shock rag parading crazies for your amusement. All of the people interviewed are looking for something very simple: a way of fighting back at a mass production consumer society that prizes standardization above all else. Through 'primitive' modifications, they are taking possession of the only thing that any of us will ever really own: our bodies."
—**WHOLE EARTH REVIEW**

"The photographs and illustrations are both explicit and astounding . . . This is the ideal biker coffee table book, a conversation piece that provides fascinating food for thought." —**IRON HORSE**

"**MODERN PRIMITIVES** approaches contemporary body adornment and ritual from the viewpoint that today's society suffers from an almost universal feeling of powerlessness to change the world, leaving the choice for exploration, individuation and primitive rite of passage to be fought out on the only ground readily available to us: our bodies."—**TIME OUT**

"In a world so badly made, as ours is, there is only one road—rebellion."
—Luis Bunuel

"Habit is probably the greatest block to seeing truth." —R.A. Schwaller de Lubicz

RE/Search #11: Pranks!

 A prank is a "trick, a mischievous act, a ludicrous act." Although not regarded as poetic or artistic acts, pranks constitute an art form and genre in themselves. Here pranksters such as Timothy Leary, Abbie Hoffman, Paul Krassner, Mark Pauline, Monte Cazazza, Jello Biafra, Earth First!, Joe Coleman, Karen Finley, Frank Discussion, John Waters and Henry Rollins challenge the sovereign authority of words, images & behavioral convention. Some tales are bizarre, as when Boyd Rice presented the First Lady with a skinned sheep's head on a platter. This iconoclastic compendium will dazzle and delight all lovers of humor, satire and irony. 8½ x 11", 240 pp, 164 photos & illustrations.

$17.99

"The definitive treatment of the subject, offering extensive interviews with 36 contemporary tricksters. . . from the Underground's answer to Studs Terkel."
—WASHINGTON POST

RE/Search #10: Incredibly Strange Films

 A guide to important territory neglected by the film criticism establishment, spotlighting unhailed directors—*Herschell Gordon Lewis, Russ Meyer, Larry Cohen, Ray Dennis Steckler, Ted V. Mikels, Doris Wishman* and others—who have been critically consigned to the ghettos of gore and sexploitation films. In-depth interviews focus on philosophy, while anecdotes entertain as well as illuminate theory. 13 interviews, numerous essays, A-Z of film personalities, "Favorite Films" list, quotations, bibliography, filmography, film synopses, & index. 8½ x 11", 224 pp. 157 photos & illustrations.

$17.99

"Flicks like these are subversive alternatives to the mind control propagated by the mainstream media."
—IRON HORSE

"Whether discussing the ethics of sex and violence on the screen, film censorship, their personal motivations, or the nuts and bolts of filmmaking from financing through distribution, the interviews are intelligent, enthusiastic and articulate."—SMALL PRESS

RE/Search #8/9: J.G. Ballard

A comprehensive special on this supremely relevant writer, now famous for *Empire of the Sun* and *Day of Creation.* W.S. Burroughs described Ballard's novel *Love & Napalm: Export U.S.A.* (1972) as "profound and disquieting...This book stirs sexual depths untouched by the hardest-core illustrated porn." 3 interviews, biography by David Pringle, fiction and non-fiction excerpts, essays, quotations, bibliography, sources, & index. 8½ x 11", 176 pp. 76 photos & illustrations by Ana Barrado, Ken Werner, Ed Ruscha, and others.

$14.99

"The RE/SEARCH to own if you must have just one . . . the most detailed, probing and comprehensive study of Ballard on the market."—BOSTON PHOENIX

"Highly recommended as both an introduction and a tribute to this remarkable writer."
—WASHINGTON POST

RE/Search #4/5: W. S. Burroughs, Brion Gysin, Throbbing Gristle

Interviews, scarce fiction, essays: this is a manual of ideas and insights. Strikingly designed, with rare photos, bibliographies, discographies, chronologies & illustrations. 7 interviews, essays, chronologies, bibliographies, discographies, sources. 8½ x 11", 100 pp. 58 photos & illustrations.

$12.99

"Interviews with pioneering cut-up artists William S. Burroughs, Brion Gysin and Throbbing Gristle . . . proposes a ground-breaking, radical cultural agenda for the '80s and '90s."—Jon Savage, LONDON OBSERVER

◆ ◆ ◆ RE/SEARCH BACKLIST ◆ ◆ ◆

RE/Search #6/7 Industrial Culture Handbook

 Essential library reference guide to the deviant performance artists and musicians of the *Industrial Culture* movement: *Survival Research Laboratories, Throbbing Gristle, Cabaret Voltaire, SPK, Non, Monte Cazazza, Johanna Went, Sordide Sentimental, R&N,* and *Z'ev.* Some topics discussed: new brain research, forbidden medical texts & films, creative crime & *interesting* criminals, modern warfare & weaponry, neglected gore films & their directors, psychotic lyrics in past pop songs, *art brut,* etc. 10 interviews, essays, quotations, chronologies, bibliographies, discographies, filmographies, sources, & index. 8½ x 11", 140 pp, 179 photos & illustrations.
$13.99

"... focuses on post-punk 'industrial' performers whose work comprises a biting critique of contemporary culture ... the book lists alone are worth the price of admission!"**—SMALL PRESS**

"A sort of subversive artists directory, profiling an interrelated group of violently imaginative creators/performers whose works blend sex, viscera, machines, crimes and/or noise ... anyone with a strong stomach, twisted imagination and hunger for alternative knowledge, take note: this could be the best $ you'll ever spend."**—TROUSER PRESS**

Trilogy: High Priest of California (novel & play); Wild Wives (novel) by Charles Willeford

 1953 San Francisco *roman noir:* the first two novels by Charles Willeford surpass the works of Jim Thompson in profundity of hard-boiled characterization, simultaneously offering a deep critique of contemporary morality. Unusual plots, tough dialogue starring anti-heroes both brutal and complex, and women living outside the lie of chivalry: *"She wasn't wearing much beneath her skirt. In an instant it was over. Fiercely and abruptly."* Plus the first publication of a play. 304 pp. 5x8". 2 introductions; bibliography; 15 photos.
$9.95

"**HIGH PRIEST OF CALIFORNIA**—The hairiest, ballsiest hard-boiled ever penned. One continuous orgy of prolonged foreplay! **WILD WIVES**—sex, schizophrenia and sadism blend into a recipe for sudden doom!"
—Dennis McMillan

"Willeford never puts a foot wrong.' **—NEW YORKER**

◆ ◆ ◆ VIDEOS & CD'S ◆ ◆ ◆

The Best of Perrey & Kingsley CD

Two fantastic, classic LPs (*The In Sound from Way Out,* and *Kaleidoscopic Vibrations*) combined on one hard-to-find, currently out-of-print CD available exclusively from Re/Search mail orders.
$16.00

Louder Faster Shorter— *Punk Video*

 One of the only surviving 16mm color documents of the original punk rock scene at the Mabuhay Gardens. 20 minute video featuring the AVENGERS, DILS, MUTANTS, SLEEPERS, and UXA. (This video is in US NTSC VHS FORMAT.)
$20.00

COMING SOON: CASSETTES & CDS OF Incredibly Strange Music

The Confessions of Wanda von Sacher-Masoch

Finally available in English: the racy and riveting *Confessions of Wanda von Sacher-Masoch*—married for ten years to Leopold von Sacher-Masoch (author of *Venus in Furs* and many other novels) whose whip-and-fur bedroom games spawned the term "masoch-ism." In this feminist classic from 100 years ago, Wanda was forced to play "sadistic" roles in Leopold's fantasies to ensure the survival of herself and her 3 children—games which called into question who was the Master and who the Slave. Besides being a compelling study of a woman's search for her own identity, strength and ultimately—complete independence—this is a true-life adventure story—an odyssey through many lands peopled by amazing characters. Underneath its unforgettable poetic imagery and almost unbearable emotional cataclysms reigns a woman's consistent unblinking investigation of the limits of morality and the deepest meanings of love. Translated by Marian Phillips, Caroline Hébert & V. Vale. 8½ x 11", 136 pages, illustrations.

$13.99

"As with all RE/Search editions, *The Confessions of Wanda von Sacher-Masoch* is extravagantly designed, in an illustrated, oversized edition that is a pleasure to hold. It is also exquisitely written, engaging and literary and turns our preconceptions upside down."—LA READER

Freaks: We Who Are Not As Others by Daniel P. Mannix

Another long out-of-print classic book based on Mannix's personal acquaintance with sideshow stars such as the Alligator Man and the Monkey Woman, etc. Read all about the notorious love affairs of midgets; the amazing story of the elephant boy; the unusual amours of Jolly Daisy, the fat woman; the famous pinhead who inspired Verdi's *Rigoletto;* the tragedy of Betty Lou Williams and her parasitic twin; the black midget, only 34 inches tall, who was happily married to a 264-pound wife; the human torso who could sew, crochet and type; and bizarre accounts of normal humans turned into freaks—either voluntarily or by evil design! 88 astounding photographs and additional material from the author's personal collection. 8½ x 11", 124pp.

$13.99

SIGNED HARDBOUND: Limited edition of 300 signed by the author on acid-free paper **$50.00**

"RE/Search has provided us with a moving glimpse at the rarified world of physical deformity; a glimpse that ultimately succeeds in its goal of humanizing the inhuman, revealing the beauty that often lies behind the grotesque and in dramatically illustrating the triumph of the human spirit in the face of overwhelming debility."
—SPECTRUM WEEKLY

The Torture Garden by Octave Mirbeau

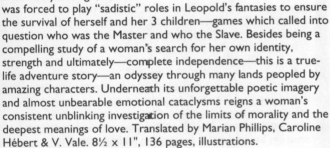

This book was once described as the "most sickening work of art of the nineteenth century!" Long out of print, Octave Mirbeau's macabre classic (1899) features a corrupt Frenchman and an insatiably cruel Englishwoman who meet and then frequent a fantastic 19th century Chinese garden where torture is practiced as an art form. The fascinating, horrific narrative slithers deep into the human spirit, uncovering murderous proclivities and demented desires. Lavish, loving detail of description. Illustrated with evocative, dream-like photos. Introduction, biography & bibliography. 8½ x 11", 120 pp, 21 photos. **$13.99**
HARDBOUND: Limited edition of 200 hardbacks on acid-free paper $29.00

". . . sadistic spectacle as apocalyptic celebration of human potential . . . A work as chilling as it is seductive."
—THE DAILY CALIFORNIAN

The Atrocity Exhibition by J.G. Ballard

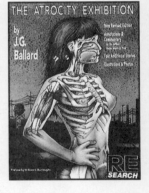

A large-format, illustrated edition of this long out-of-print classic, widely regarded as Ballard's finest, most complex work. Withdrawn by E.P. Dutton after having been shredded by Doubleday, this outrageous work was finally printed in a small edition by Grove before lapsing out of print 15 years ago. With 4 additional fiction pieces, extensive annotations (a book in themselves), disturbing photographs by Ana Barrado and dazzling, anatomically explicit medical illustrations by Phoebe Gloeckner. 8½ x 11", 136pp.

$13.99

SIGNED HARDBOUND: Limited Edition of 300 signed by the author on acid-free paper **$50.00**

"*The Atrocity Exhibition* is remarkably fresh. One does not read these narratives as one does other fiction . . . one enters into them as a kind of ritual . . ."
—SAN FRANCISCO CHRONICLE

RE/SEARCH BACKLIST

RE/Search #1-2-3

Deep into the heart of the Control Process. Preoccupation: Creativity & Survival, past, present & future. These are the early tabloid issues, 11x17", full of photos & innovative graphics.

◆ **#1** J.G. Ballard, Cabaret Voltaire, Julio Cortazar, Octavio Paz, Sun Ra, *The Slits*, Robert K. Brown (editor, *Soldier of Fortune), Non,* Conspiracy Theory Guide, Punk Prostitutes, and more.

◆ **#2** *DNA,* James Blood Ulmer, *Z'ev,* Aboriginal Music, West African Music Guide, Surveillance Technology, Monte Cazazza on poisons, Diane Di Prima, Seda, German Electronic Music Chart, Isabelle Eberhardt, and more.

◆ **#3** Fela, New Brain Research, The Rattlesnake Man, Sordide Sentimental, New Guinea, Kathy Acker, Sado-Masochism (interview with Pat Califia); Joe Dante, Johanna Went, *SPK, Flipper,* Physical Modification of Women, and more.

$8.00 each.

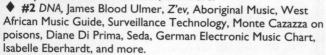

SET OF RE/SEARCH 1-2-3: $17.99

"Who wishes to be creative, must first destroy and smash accepted values."
—Nietzsche

Search & Destroy:

Incendiary interviews, passionate photographs, art brutal. Corrosive minimalist documentation of the only youth rebellion of the seventies: punk rock (1977-78). The philosophy and culture, BEFORE the mass media takeover and inevitable cloning.

◆ **#1** Premiere issue. Crime, Nuns, Global Punk Survey.

◆ **#2** Devo, Clash, Ramones, Iggy, Weirdos, Patti Smith, Vivienne Westwood, Avengers, Dils, etc.

◆ **#3** Devo, Damned, Patti Smith, Avengers, Tom Verlaine, Capt. Beefheart, Blondie, Residents, Alternative TV, Throbbing Gristle.

◆ **#4** Iggy, Dead Boys, Bobby Death, Jordan & the Ants, Mumps, Metal Urbain, Helen Wheels, Sham 69, Patti Smith.

◆ **#5** Sex Pistols, Nico, Crisis, Screamers, Suicide, Crime, Talking Heads, Anarchy, Surrealism & New Wave essay.

◆ **#6** Throbbing Gristle, Clash, Nico, Talking Heads, Pere Ubu, Nuns, UXA, Negative Trend, Mutants, Sleepers, Buzzcocks.

◆ **#7** John Waters, Devo, DNA, Cabaret Voltaire, Roky Erickson, Clash, Amos Poe, Mick Farren, Offs, Vermilion & more.

◆ **#8** Mutants, Dils, Cramps, Devo, Siouxsie, Chrome, Pere Ubu, Judy Nylon & Patti Palladin, Flesheaters, Offs, Weirdos, etc.

◆ **#9** Dead Kennedys, Rockabilly Rebels, X, Winston Tong, David Lynch, Television, Pere Ubu, DOA, etc.

◆ **#10** J.G. Ballard, William S. Burroughs, Feederz, Plugz, X, Russ Meyer, Steve Jones, etc. Reprinted by Demand!

◆ **#11** The all photo supplement. Black and White.

$4.00 each.

SEARCH & DESTROY: COMPLETE SET ISSUES #1-11 for only $39.00.

T-SHIRTS

Ask us for our current catalog of T-Shirts

BOOKS DISTRIBUTED BY RE/SEARCH

Body Art

 From England, a glossy 8½ x 11" magazine devoted to tattoo, piercing, body painting, tribal influences, pubic hairdressing, et al. Outstanding explicit Color/B&W photographs, instructive text—a beautiful production. Approx. 48 pgs.

$17.00 EACH

ISSUE #1:	Finally back in print! Mr Sebastian, Scythian Man.
ISSUE #2:	Pubic Hairdressing, Out of the Closet, Shotsie.
ISSUE #3:	Africa. Adorned, Tanta, Nipple Jewelry.
ISSUE #4:	Tattoo Expo '88, Tribal Influence, Male Piercings.
ISSUE #5:	Female Piercings, The Year of the Snake.
ISSUE #6:	Body Painting, Celtic Tattoos.
ISSUE #7:	Female Nipple Development, Plastic Bodies.
ISSUE #8:	Tattoo Symbolism, Piercing Enlargement.
ISSUE #9:	Tattoos, Nipple Piercing, The Perfect Body.
ISSUE #10:	Amsterdam Tattoo Convention, Cliff Raven.
ISSUE #11:	Ed Hardy, Fred Corbin, Beyond The Pain Barrier.
ISSUE #12:	Tattoo Expo '90, Genital Modifications.
ISSUE #13:	New Orleans Tattoo Convention 1990.
ISSUE #14:	Krystyne Kolorful, Paris Tattoo Convention.
ISSUE #15:	The Stainless Steel Ball, Bodyshots: Richard Todd
ISSUE #16:	Tattoo Expo '91, Indian Hand Painting, Nail Tattoos.

Please list an alternate title for all Body Art selections.

TattooTime
edited by Don Ed Hardy

◆ **#1: NEW TRIBALISM.**
This classic issue features the new "tribal" tattooing renaissance started by Cliff Raven, Ed Hardy, Leo Zulueta & others.
$10.00

◆ **#2: TATTOO MAGIC.**
This issue examines all facets of Magic & the Occult.
$10.00

◆ **#3: MUSIC & SEA TATTOOS.**
Deluxe double book issue with over 300 photos.
$15.00

◆ **#4: LIFE & DEATH.**
Deluxe double book issue with fantastic photos, examining trademarks, architectural and mechanical tattoos, the Eternal Spiral, a Tattoo Museum, plus the gamut of Death imagery.
$15.00

◆ **#5: ART FROM THE HEART.**
All *NEW* issue that's bigger than ever before (128 pgs) with hundreds of color photographs. Featuring in-depth articles on tattooers, contemporary tattooing in Samoa, a survey of the new weirdo monster tattoos and much more!
$20.00

PopVoid #1: '60s Culture.
edited by Jim Morton

Edited by Jim Morton (who guest-edited *Incredibly Strange Films*). Fantastic anthology of neglected pop culture: Lawrence Welk, Rod McKuen, Paper Dresses, Nudist Colonies, Goofy Grape, etc. 8½ x 11", 100 pp.
$9.95

Halloween by Ken Werner

A classic photo book. Startling photographs from the "Mardi Gras of the West," San Francisco's *adult* Halloween festivities in the Castro district. Limited supply. Beautiful 9x12" hardback bound in black boards. 72 pgs. Black glossy paper.
$11.00

◆ S P E C I A L   D I S C O U N T S ◆

Special Deluxe Offer (Save $80!)
Complete set of RE/Search serials plus reprints and complete set of Search & Destroy.

Offer includes Re/Search #1-2-3 tabloids, #4/5 Burroughs/Gysin/Throbbing Gristle, #6/7 Industrial Culture Handbook, #8/9 J.G. Ballard, #10 Incredibly Strange Films, #11 Pranks!, #12 Modern Primitives, #13: Angry Women, Search & Destroy Issues #1-11, The Confessions of Wanda von Sacher-Masoch, Freaks: We Who Are Not As Others, The Atrocity Exhibition, Torture Garden, the Willeford Trilogy and Me & Big Joe.
Special Discount Offer: $200 ppd. Seamail/Canada: $220. AIR Europe: $307. AIR Austr./Japan: $346.
FOR *RE/Search #14: Incredibly Strange Music* ADD ONLY $10.

> **PRICES FOR THE SPECIAL DISCOUNT OFFERS INCLUDE SHIPPING & HANDLING!**

Special Discount Offer (Save $45!)
Complete set of all RE/Search serials

Offer includes the Re/Search #1-2-3 tabloids, #4/5 Burroughs/Gysin/Throbbing Gristle, #6/7 Industrial Culture Handbook, #8/9 J.G. Ballard, #10 Incredibly Strange Films, #11 Pranks!, #12 Modern Primitives, and #13 Angry Women.
Special Discount Offer Only: $110 ppd. Seamail/Canada: $120. AIR Europe: $176. AIR Austr/Japan: $200.
FOR *RE/Search #14: Incredibly Strange Music* ADD ONLY $10.

Special Reprints Offer (Save $20!)
Complete set of all RE/Search Classics

Offer includes the Willeford Trilogy, Freaks: We Who Are Not As Others, The Torture Garden, The Atrocity Exhibition, and The Confessions of Wanda von Sacher-Masoch.
Special Discount Offer: $58 ppd. Seamail/Canada: $60. AIR Europe: $85. AIR Austr/Japan $96.

Subscribe to RE/Search:

REGULAR SUBSCRIPTION:
You will receive the next three books published by RE/Search which will include either our numbered interview format serials or Re/Search classics. **$40.**

INSTITUTION SUBSCRIPTION:
Sorry no library or university subscriptions. Please place individual orders from this catalog.

SUBSCRIPTIONS SENT SURFACE MAIL ONLY! NO AIRMAIL.

Do you know someone who would like our catalog? Write name & address below.

NAME

ADDRESS

CITY, STATE, ZIP

PLEASE SEE PREVIOUS PAGE FOR SPECIAL DISCOUNTS

◆ ◆ ◆ ORDER FORM ◆ ◆ ◆

HAVE YOU ORDERED FROM US BEFORE?   circle one   **YES   NO**

NAME

ADDRESS

CITY, STATE, ZIP

Order by mail or phone: Phone orders may be placed Monday through Friday, from 10 a.m. to 6 p.m. Pacific Standard Time.
Phone #415-362-1465

Check or Money Order Enclosed (Payable to RE/Search Publications) or

VISA/MasterCard #

Exp. Date _____   Signature: _____

MAIL TO: RE/SEARCH PUBLICATIONS
20 ROMOLO ST., #B
SAN FRANCISCO, CA 94133

TITLE	QUANTITY	TOTAL
Subtotal		
CA Residents (add 8½% Sales Tax)		
Shipping/Handling (except Special Discounts)		
Add $3 UPS (Continental U.S. only)		
TOTAL DUE		

SHIPPING & HANDLING CHARGES

First item $4. Add $1 per each additional item. For UPS add $3 (flat rate per order). You must give a street address—no **PO Box** addresses.

INTERNATIONAL CUSTOMERS. For SEAMAIL: first item $6; add $2 per each additional item. **For AIRMAIL:** first item $15; add $12 per each additonal item.

ATTENTION CANADIAN CUSTOMERS: WE DO NOT ACCEPT PERSONAL CHECKS EVEN IF IT IS FROM A U.S. DOLLAR ACCOUNT. SEND INTERNATIONAL MONEY ORDERS ONLY! (available from the post office.)

SEND SASE FOR CATALOG (or 4 IRCs for OVERSEAS) FOR INFORMATION CALL: (415) 362-1465

PAYMENT IN U.S. DOLLARS ALLOW 6-8 WEEKS FOR DELIVERY